ELEMENTS OF

Turning Bowls and Platters

Selected Readings from *American Woodturner*,
journal of the American Association of Woodturners

American Association of Woodturners
222 Landmark Center
75 5th St. W
St. Paul, MN 55102-7704
877-595-9094
www.woodturner.org

Contents

Published by American Association of Woodturners,
222 Landmark Center, 75 5th St. W., St. Paul, MN 55102-7704.
877-595-9094, www.woodturner.org.

American Woodturner (ISSN 0895-9005) is published bimonthly
by American Association of Woodturners.

Turning Bowls and Platters
ISBN 978-1-939662-08-8

Printed on Demand in United States of America
American Association of Woodturners, www.woodturner.org

Introduction

The simple wooden bowl endlessly fascinates today's woodturners, so much that our contemporary craft centers on bowl-turning in its infinite variations. Here are a few of the reasons why:

- You can make a bowl from any kind of wood, whether it comes from the lumber yard or from a downed tree in your own back yard.
- Turning fresh-cut wood is an exhilarating experience as fat wet shavings fly off the blank and ribbon into the air. It's fun.
- Compared to other woodcrafts, turning a bowl is quick to learn and quick to do, even as it contain a lifetime of nuanced skill to be practiced and acquired.
- Everyone loves the natural beauty of wood. A wooden bowl you made yourself is an extraordinary gift for anyone, for any occasion.
- People ate from wooden bowls and platters for eons before china was invented, and you can too. Wooden bowls are useful.
- Contemporary wood art centers on turnings that are decorated and embellished for artistic expression. Turned wood makes a superb canvas for art.
- The simple wooden bowl, cradled in two hands and presented to another, confirms the ancient human rituals of offering and receiving.

The stories in this book have been chosen not only to help you get started in this fascinating craft, but also to deepen your own skills and expand your creative horizons.

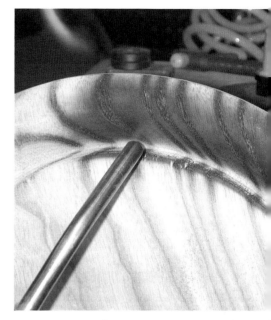

Selected Readings from *AW Journal*

From its founding in 1986, the American Association of Woodturners has published a regular journal of advice, information, and good fellowship for everyone interested in the field. Led by a series of dedicated editors and board members, the *AW Journal* has evolved to become *American Woodturner* magazine, now published in full color six times each year.

The *AW Journal* is a genuine treasure-trove of practical, shop-tested information written by woodturners for their fellow woodturners. *Turning Bowls and Platters* is part of an ongoing series being extracted from this archive. *Turning Bowls and Platters* is available as a 64-page printed book, or as a digital ebook that is readable on all your electronic devices.

Safe woodturning is fun woodturning. A little time spent with this book will help you build strong skills at the lathe while teaching you best woodturning practices.

Twenty Ways Not to Turn a Bowl

Nick Cook

When it was suggested that I write this article, I wondered if it was because someone thought I didn't know how to turn a bowl. I was assured that I drew this assignment not because I'm inexperienced at bowl turning but rather because I have had so many woodturning students.

I have been teaching woodturning for more than 20 years, and many of the classes have been basic, for beginners, or an introduction to woodturning. You can ask anyone who has been involved in one of these classes and they will tell you that my most frequently used direction is: "Stop, don't do that!"

Anyone who teaches basics at John C. Campbell, Appalachian Craft Center, Arrowmont, or Anderson Ranch Craft Center expects to have raw beginners in a class. We also expect novices with just a little experience and even expect a few who have been turning for a number of years.

The teacher's challenge is getting all of the students on the same page in the same book at the same time. Adult learners seem to have their own ideas about how to turn, and some are not the least interested in how I want them to turn. Some are self-taught; some

No matter how eager you are to turn your first "keeper," don't begin turning with large or expensive stock. The 8"-diameter stock on the headstock is more appropriate.

Photos: Marisa Pruss

have attended other classes. Others have read woodturning books and watched videos.

And others...must have been time-traveling to their eighth-grade shop classes when someone was attempting to instruct them.

The right stock

One of the biggest problems teachers face is that many students are itching to turn a really large bowl the first time they step up to the lathe. Or, they lug in something that cost them big bucks.

Stop! Don't do that!

1 Too big. You will learn a lot more about turning techniques by turning lots of small, shallow bowls than you ever will by turning one or two really large pieces.

2 Too valuable. Whatever you do, do not pay fo;r practice wood. There is plenty of free wood out there—the stuff really does grow on trees. Ask around at your AAW chapter; you'll find a resourceful group with plenty of practice pieces.

3 Too hard. Green wood is a great way to start. Wood lots and local tree cutters are great sources for practice materials.

4 Too deep. Start out with a small (8"-diameter) platter before attempting any type of bowl. When you are comfortable with that, transition to a shallow bowl—just slightly deeper, but still about 8" in diameter.

Keep the form open rather than making the openings smaller. The smaller the opening, the harder it is to cut the interior.

5 Not ready for prime time, (or finish). Don't worry about applying finish to anything—that will come later. Think practice pieces. I suggest that you use a screw chuck or faceplate and turn shapes that resemble bowl forms until you get to the point of becoming comfortable with the bowl gouge. When you get to where you do not have to think about what the tool is doing, you are ready to turn a bowl. Once you get a few decent-looking forms, turn the bowl around and begin hollowing the interior. Then, get out the finish.

The right speed

Too often, novice woodturners go from turning spindles to turning bowls without adjusting the lathe speed. Too big and too fast is a deadly combination.

Here's a good habit to develop: Before you turn on your lathe, always stand to the left or right of the chuck.

Stop! Don't do that!

6 Too much speed. Before mounting stock between centers or on a faceplate or chuck, switch on the lathe without anything mounted. This will give you the opportunity to see where the speed was set when the lathe was last used. Developing this habit will prevent an accident.

I encourage students to reduce the speed of their machines at the end of every turning session. This is easy on variable-speed lathes, but I meet resistance to this when students are learning on machines with step pulleys. Do it anyway; it's never too early to develop good safety habits.

7 Too much of a hurry. Another problem that can ruin your day occurs when you have a large piece on the lathe and stop the machine too quickly. This happened to my friend Andy Marinos, who suggested adding this tip to the Don't Do! list.

To turn the bottom of a bowl, Andy mounted his large flat jaws on his scroll chuck and mounted the rim of the bowl in the jaws. Without checking the speed, he turned on the lathe. It was going much too fast for the task at hand. Andy quickly hit the stop button on the machine, and the motor stopped. But, the chuck and the bowl had enough momentum to keep spinning—even with the lathe stopped. When it came off the spindle, the assembly caught his hand between it and the tool rest. Andy's wound required numerous stitches.

Here's a safer plan: Start the lathe at a low speed or use the setscrew in the chuck to lock it onto the spindle.

8 Standing in the wrong place. You should always stand to one side of the workpiece (out of the path of the spinning blank) when you turn on your lathe as shown in the photo.

The right tool

Before anyone stands in front of a lathe, I review all of the tools, their uses, and how to sharpen each. I identify each tool, explain how it is used, show how to sharpen it, and also show the various cuts that can be made. I also explain what each tool is not designed to do. But sometimes, that's not enough.

Stop! Don't do that!

9 **No roughing-out gouge for bowl work.** For bowl turning, never turn with a roughing gouge. This should be a no-brainer, but I have seen it done. In my mind, this tool should be referred to as a spindle roughing gouge.

Here's a classic example. One student mounted a large, square blank on a lightweight lathe and turned it on at too high of speed. Needless to say, I screamed from across the room, "Stop, don't do that!" When I got to where he was working, I also discovered that he was about to attack the piece with a 1¼" spindle roughing gouge. Oh, and it wasn't sharpened yet; it had just come out of the box.

You should not use the skew on a bowl either!

10 **Big gap at tool rest.** One of the most common problems is extending the tool too far out over the tool rest. Many times, students will continue cutting without moving the rest any closer to the blank. Once the tool extends more than 1" or so beyond the rest, stop the machine and move the tool rest closer. Lathe tools have been known to break over the tool rest—a very bad thing.

The height of the tool rest is determined by the tool you are using and your height and stance. Always place the tool on the rest first, touch the back of the tool to the blank, then gently lift the tool handle until

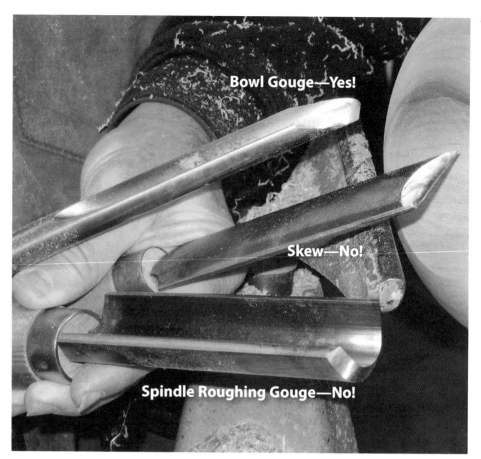

The bowl gouge, top, is the only one of the three lathe tools you should use for your bowl projects.

As your bowl takes shape, stop the lathe frequently and move the tool rest to about 1" from the stock.

the bevel makes contact with the wood. This will ensure the bevel supports the cutting edge. You will be less likely to get catches this way.

11 **Moving tool rest with lathe running.** Don't even think about it! Never move the tool rest with the lathe running.

12 **Not following the curve.** It is not uncommon for a beginner to make straight cuts along the length of the tool rest, correctly move the rest closer but continue to cut in a straight line. To produce better profiles, move the tool rest around the shape of the bowl. The result is a cone-shaped bowl. This is where a curved tool rest can be helpful, although not a necessity.

Work on a continuous curve—not thinness.

13 **Wrong direction.** For face-grain bowls, cut uphill or from bottom to top on the exterior of the bowl. On the interior of your bowl, cut downhill or from the rim to the center.

14 **No body movement.** You are not bolted to the floor. To produce better curves, use your body and move it through an arch. Learn that "woodturner's sway."

Place the tool handle against your hip and hold the handle with your right hand near the shaft and your left hand on the tool rest. Keep your left hand on the tool rest throughout the cut to provide additional support. Remember, if you move your feet, you move the pivot and lose the curve. Learn to swing your body, but don't move your feet.

15 **Dull tools.** Beginners also have a problem determining whether a tool is sharp or not. It takes experience to be able to tell. Different woods react differently to being cut. Most beginners merely increase pressure as the cutting edge gets dull. This can be dangerous.

When turning the outside of a face-grain bowl, turn from the bottom to the top (sometimes described as uphill).

When you remove stock from the interior of a face-grain bowl, always begin at the rim and work toward the center (also described as downhill).

When in doubt, sharpen the tool. And, the best way to sharpen a tool for beginners is with jigs and fixtures; they all work, and they all provide excellent results. Hand-sharpening also works after you learn what you are doing, but the jigs and fixtures will provide consistent results each and every time.

Be sure to touch up your edge on the grinder before making your final cut. A dull tool will pull or tear at the fibers, leaving a surface that you can't sand smooth. This is especially true on end grain.

Each instructor will show you his or her favorite grind for the bowl gouge. They all work if you take the time to learn how to use them. It is more important that you learn to consistently reproduce the grind you are using than which profile you choose.

Grinding by hand is important to learn, but for the beginner, jigs and fixtures are a great help.

16 **Too much pressure.** Another common problem is applying too much pressure when cutting the surface. This will force the heel of the tool into the surface and bruise the fibers, leaving lines that remain invisible until you apply finish. Yikes!

These lines are almost impossible to sand away. You must recut the surface. Relax and let the cutting edge do the work rather than forcing it.

The right mount

A lot of bowl-turning problems begin with how the material is attached to the lathe. Because every new lathe is shipped with a faceplate, this is the obvious choice for the beginning woodturner.

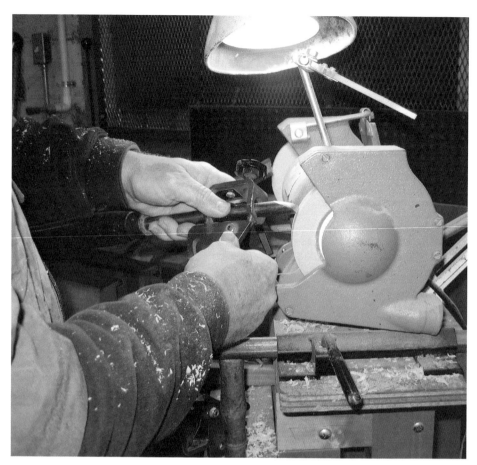

A grinding jig helps many new turners repeat the same bevel on a lathe tool.

Stop! Don't do that!

17 **Wrong screws.** Trouble can begin at the first step when you screw the blank to the faceplate. Here, several problems can occur. It usually starts with drywall screws; they are too thin and too brittle. You exacerbate the problem when you draw up drywall screws with a power screwdriver, which pulls them up tight and snaps them.

Sheet metal screws are a better choice to attach turning stock to a faceplate. These screws are case-hardened and have deeper and sharper threads. Make sure you choose a length that is appropriate. Square-drive screws are also popular and are much easier to remove from hardwood.

For securing turning stock, one size does not fit all. For an 8"-diameter blank that is up to about 2" thick, I recommend #8×3/4" screws. For a 14×8" blank, secure with #14×1-1/2" hardened screws.

18 **Difficult grain.** You must also consider the material you will be putting the screws into. End grain requires larger and longer screws. Beware of punky or spalted woods; once the wood has started to decay, it is extremely difficult to get a screw to hold.

Sapwood does not hold screws as well as heartwood. To be on the safe side, bring up the tailstock with a live center for insurance. This will give additional support if the screws do not hold.

Choose turning stock that offers a better chance for success. Dale Nish says it best: "Life is too short to turn crappy wood!"

19 **Poor grip.** Once you get excited about turning, it probably won't be long before you purchase a 4-jaw scroll chuck, which I think holds material better on the lathe. However, this chuck has its own set of challenges.

I have had many instances where students have made tenons too small or the recesses too shallow. Either case can cause the blank to separate from the chuck.

Punky wood and sapwood present the same challenges and grain problems as noted above.

20 **Loose fit.** Green wood requires you to tighten the jaws of the chuck repeatedly as moisture is forced from the blank. Just as with the faceplate, remember to use the tailstock and center whenever possible.

Turn safely and have fun. But by all means, think about what you are doing and consider the risks involved. If you are unsure, ask someone with more experience. If it looks dangerous, it probably is.

"Stop, don't do that!"

Nick Cook (nickcook@earthlink.net) is an American Woodturner contributing editor. Nick, who lives in Marietta, Georgia, will teach afternoons in the Youth Turning Room at the AAW symposium in Louisville.

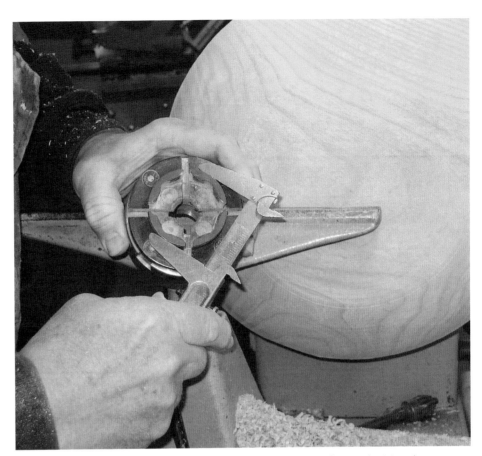

If you want your bowl to stay in the chuck, you'll learn the value of properly sizing the tenon. If the chuck loosens, the bowl will fly out off the lathe.

Sheet-metal screws should be your only choice for mounting turning stock to faceplates. You can see how a drywall screw can break off, which leads to huge safety issues.

Bowl Turning System

Luke Mann

One of the wonderful things about woodturning is that it is so varied in its applications, its interpretations, and its expressions. The same goes for all of the steps I use in my woodturning business. They are a system, but a flexible and responsive one, assembled from my own experiences and gleanings from others. My hope is that there might be something here for many of you.

I began turning professionally after taking a three-day woodturning course with David Ellsworth in February 1992. Before that I had been an admirer of turned wood, which I had seen on various occasions, most memorably in travels through New Zealand and Australia in 1987–88. At that time my own turning experience

consisted of three weeks back in junior high school. I approach the lathe as a means to remove material quickly while shaping beautiful forms, both functional and sculptural. For me, the natural choice has been to work with wet, unseasoned wood (the state in which I usually find it), allowing it to contribute changes in shape through drying. I regard this as a dynamic collaboration with a living material. I turn from 160 to 180 pieces a year. I sell half of these wholesale to galleries, a quarter on consignment, and the remaining quarter directly to private customers and collectors.

I think of my work as divided into six phases, from locating material for turning to delivering completed work.

1. Gathering material

Finding and gathering materials is an ongoing project. Just when I think I have a relationship established with a logger (he has an idea of what I am looking for, and I know what he requires to keep him calling me with a find) he shifts to cutting only softwoods or dried flowers. So I find myself looking for loggers as much as looking for wood. Living in Vermont has worked well for me in this regard. The local wood supply is rich with maple, cherry, ash, red and white oak, elm and birch. Last January, when I was supposed to be writing this article, we had a major ice storm, and I couldn't sit still. I was out there gathering downed wood—apple, honey locust, and sycamore—some wonderful finds!

As I am not a production turner, my needs for twelve months of turning might look something like this:

• A couple of large 30-inch-diameter curly lumpy maple butt logs, 12-feet long, delivered from a nearby logging site.

• Two or three cherry trees around 16 inches at chest height, twisted specimens leaning threateningly over a local farmer's fence line.

• A dozen or so decent size burls, 12 to 20 inches in diameter, mostly located by logger acquaintances who spend their days in the woods and therefore have ample opportunity to come across these abnormalities.

• Plus, the odd fruit tree or some such prize I get tipped off to

Figure 1: Author's wood storage area protects his stock from sun, rain, and snow. Maple and burl blocks are stacked off the ground and in shavings for a moist environment that forestalls checking and promotes spalting.

AW 13:1, p12

Figure 2

Bandsaw jig

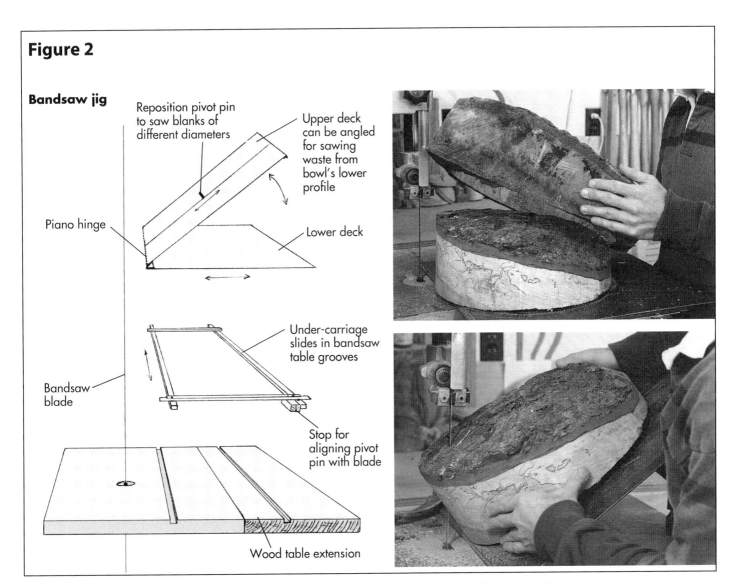

Figure 2: Author's bandsaw jig provides a safe and efficient way to prepare flat-topped turning blanks. Begin by drilling a 1/2" hole in the approximate center of the blank to accommodate the jig's pivot pin. Place the blank on the jig and, with the upper deck of the jig flat, rotate the blank through the blade to produce a disk. Then shift the pin to the right (away from the blade), raise and prop the upper deck, and saw around again to shape what will be the lower profile of the bowl.

or simply spot myself and add to my store. I take logs in the longest lengths manageable so as to limit end waste. It is helpful to leave 6 to 10 inches extending from either end of a burl to help keep large cracks from entering the burl.

The single biggest requirement to finding material is relationships. And I very much enjoy this aspect of my work, as it allows me to get out, interact, and communicate with many and various sorts of people. Relationships with land-owners, loggers, farmers, tree service people, all mean opportunities to obtain material whether by purchase or barter.

2. Storing and stockpiling

Once I have acquired the material, I need to consider how I will store it until I can get it to the lathe. I have learned that different woods keep differently. As a rule I wax the ends of logs and burls. Cherry, which doesn't spalt or improve with time, is best if used rather quickly. The creamy sapwood turns an unpleasant green-brown, so I try to use cherry within two to four months, and I leave it in log form until it is turning time.

I prefer to sit on maple a while to encourage spalting. I store the logs up off the ground (same as for burls) in a shady spot for a year or two. If no shade is available or if a lot of the bark is missing, I move directly to cutting up the log.

When I cut into a log or burl, I commit to cutting it up in its entirety, reading the wood all the

Figure 3a: Turning the blank begins between centers.
Figure 3b: Once the blank is roughly shaped, proportion, figure, and special features are considered in sketching a design.
Figure 3c: After finishing the outside, the blank is remounted in a four-jaw chuck for hollowing.
Figure 3d: A cone is removed beginning with a parting cut along the bowl wall.
Figure 3e: A wooden wedge breaks the cone free. The cone can be used to turn a smaller bowl.

while, determining where the bowls and vessels lie. Checking is an enemy, and cracks will enter end grain quickly if allowed to, drastically reducing the usable material.

After cutting up maple or burl, I quickly pack away the resulting blocks in shavings from turning and cover them with plastic. I built a simple shed with four stalls, 4 x 8 feet, and a roof to fend off the summer sun and maintain a moist environment for the blocks. In this way checking is discouraged and spalting is encouraged, which is fine by me. Material stored thus is like money in the bank, and affords me the freedom to work material needing more immediate attention—a small apple crotch, for instance, which if left unturned would self-destruct.

3. Prepping for the lathe

When I'm ready to turn, which I try to do three solid days a week, I prepare wood for the lathe in one of two ways. If it is a flat-topped block for a straightforward open form, I take it to my bandsaw jig. For all others—lidded vessels, hollow forms, live-edged turnings—I do my best with the chainsaw to remove corners and arrive at some semblance of a

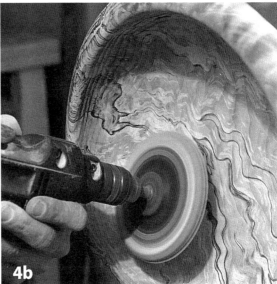

Figure 4a: The interior is shaped in a series of passes with the bowl gouge.
Figure 4b: The interior is sanded in the same manner as the outside, using a foam-backed sanding disc, first with the work under power, then with the work stationary.
Figure 4c: The hollowed bowl is inverted onto a foam-clad spigot and held in place by the tailstock while the foot is shaped.
Figure 4d. Finish is applied as soon as the bowl comes off the lathe.

round "balanced" form, just prior to turning.

I designed my bandsaw jig to safely and efficiently prepare blanks for the lathe. It consists of an upper deck with a pivot pin, hinged to a lower deck, which rides on an under-carriage that slides in my bandsaw-table slots. I begin by drilling a hole approximately in the center of the block to receive the jig's pivot pin. With the block on the jig, the upper deck flat on the lower deck, and the saw running, I slide the jig forward, the block into the blade, and rotate the block to remove the corners. This gives me a first glance at the beauty within while producing a round blank for turning.

In preparation for the second cut, I remove the blank from the jig and shift the pin to the right, away from the blade, so that the blank's edge will be even with the piano-hinged edge of the jig. I then raise and prop the jig's upper deck at a 30- to 45-degree angle, and slide the whole thing forward into the blade, trimming waste from what will be the lower sides of the bowl.

I will prepare as many as twelve such blanks at once, storing them in a closed box for up to a couple of weeks before turning them.

4. Turning

I next mount the prepared blank on the lathe between centers. This allows me a lot of freedom to adjust my axes in response to the material while removing bark and irregularities. I choose to do most of the turning with 1/2-inch deep-fluted bowl gouges ground to a few different profiles.

At this point I pause to consider my design, taking into account the patterns of color and figure and any remaining voids or irregularities. After shaping and refining, I sand the exterior using a simple foam-backed power disc system. I leave a clean, round tenon below the bowl's foot to grip the blank in my four-jaw chuck for hollowing.

I mount the blank in the chuck and remove a cone from the bowl's interior as follows: I use a homemade parting tool and, entering near the rim, I cut straight in toward the foot of the bowl, stopping at sufficient depth — experience helps here. I stop the lathe and drive a wood wedge in to separate the cone from the blank, splitting the remaining 2 to 3 inches at the bottom of the cone. Removing the cone this way saves me time and the cone itself can be used for a small turning.

I complete the hollowing of the piece to the desired thickness and depth with a sharp gouge. To sand the interior I cut down (on the lathe) the rubber disc backing plate to enable the disc to conform to the concave surface. If sandpaper loads up with damp particles, I use a small brass or stainless brush for cleaning the abrasive without contaminating the wet wood. Mirka Abrasives offers an excellent sandpaper, superior to others I've used. I get it from a local auto supply distributor. I use their 5-inch adhesive sanding discs and find they are fast and durable, and hold up well to moisture.

I invert the hollowed bowl onto a foam-clad spigot and hold it in place with the tailstock. I remove the tenon, and shape the foot, hollowing the area inside the foot to a thickness consistent with the rest of the bowl.

5. Finishing and drying

Immediately upon removal from the lathe, the bowl gets a liberal application of a food-safe oil finish.

Figure 5: Author uses slotted drying shelves in his basement shop. A bowl comes off the lathe, is finished, and is placed on the lowest shelf first. Gradually it is moved up the shelves and re-oiled as the surface calls for. Final drying takes place on shelves in his living room.

Figure 6: Spalted yellow birch burl, 14" dia.

I use Bioshield Primer Oil followed by Meldos Hard Oil. These products are totally food-safe and wonderful to work with.

I place the piece on a set of slatted drying shelves, initially on the bottom shelf nearest the cool, concrete basement floor. Over the course of the next two to three weeks, depending on shape and thickness, I elevate the bowl gradually up the shelves, for controlled drying. I apply oil periodically as the surface calls for it, always taking care to wipe away excess once the oil becomes tacky. The final drying occurs over another two to three weeks on shelves on our living room walls. When I am satisfied that a piece has ceased its movement (no complex methods here of weighing and recording; experience and a conservative approach has taught me), I flatten its bottom against a disc on the lathe. My final touch is to sign the piece (woodburning my name, the year, and the wood, and carving my logo), apply an oil-and-beeswax mix, and wet-sand with 600- or 800-grit, wiping the excess.

6. Marketing and sales

According to my wife, and CFO, these steps are the most critical. I like Ron Kent's approach to pricing, which I paraphrase here: Simply consider what this turning is worth to you. Establish an amount that you would be satisfied to receive in exchange for the piece, less than which, you'd prefer to keep the piece. Then put the work out there for sale. If it sells, great! If it doesn't, reconsider your marketing strategy or seek another source of income.

Initially, though, pricing may simply reflect the time and materials you have in a piece. Try and determine what hourly rate you need to earn. As your work is accepted into better galleries, is being received well (selling), and improves, then raise your prices incrementally.

To get your work into galleries I encourage you to do what I did. Turn the best work you are able to today, then photograph it. Most galleries want digital images. Learn what you can about photographing your work. Pool your resources. Make use of any friends, neighbors, or relatives that have expertise in this area. Set aside a place and some time to improve your photography. Establish some known conditions—like background, lighting, camera placement,and exposure—then study and rework the results with these in mind. Once you get decent results, fine-tune them.

With your good photographs, make a list of shops and galleries where you would like to see your work on display, learn what their application requirements are, and apply. As you get accepted, value these relationships, even if the gallery was not your first choice.

I currently have a combination of wholesale and consignment arrangements with galleries. This works well, as the wholesale accounts offer a scheduled payday, thirty days from delivery, while the others pay sporadically or seasonally, when work is sold.

When it comes to delivery time, whether to a gallery or an individual, I am careful to keep detailed records. For this I use a basic, carbonless invoice book that produces three copies (one for invoicing, one for shipping, and one for my files), recording name, address, date, a description of the work (including wood, dimensions, and a sketch of the profile), and price.

I get the heaviest boxes I can find for shipping. I carefully separate bowls with paper, bubble wrap, whatever is available, keeping newsprint and colored paper out of contact with the work. Then I float these securely nested bowls or individual pieces in foam peanuts or wadded paper. I include an invoice in the box with addresses, etc. Tape well and label clearly. I use UPS and the U.S. Mail. I always insure for the amount I would receive whether wholesale, consignment percentage, or retail.

This system works for me. I hope you can find something useful here to apply to your own work.

Luke Mann lives and works in Waitsfield, VT.

Bottom Thickness

Dick Powell

For a long time, I've struggled with not knowing the exact thickness of the bottom of a bowl as I turn and shape the inside. Using a pencil gives a good eyeball approximation. Calipers are okay; however, if there is a significant amount of wood left on the outside or if I'm not sure yet what the foot will look like, calipers are no better than a good approximation.

A couple years ago, I came up with a foolproof method that is precise. Since then, I have yet to make a funnel out of what was supposed to be a bowl.

I turn on a OneWay 24/36 lathe, but this method should work on any lathe.

Make a block of wood

The key is to make two blocks of wood that will be placed in between the ways of your lathe, next to its headstock. Cut the lengths to exactly the distance measured from some known and fixed point. In my case, I use the base of the headstock, which is firmly and permanently attached to the lathe's bed. Cut the wood so that it fits on the lathe's bed and does not fall off (*Figure 1*).

For the first block: If a bowl is attached to the lathe with the foot/tenon in the scroll chuck (*Figure 2*), set a square on the lathe's bed and flush against the face of the chuck's jaws. The length of the block is exactly the distance from the base of the headstock to the square.

For the second block: If using jumbo jaws to finish the foot (*Figure 3*), this distance is probably not the same as the first block. Set the square flush against the face of the jumbo jaws. The length of the block is exactly the distance from the base of the headstock to the square.

The precise length of each block is critical. Be sure to note on each block which set of jaws it fits.

To use the block for measuring

With the bowl's foot/tenon held by the chuck, simply put the first block on the lathe's bed, flush against the headstock. Set the square on the lathe a convenient distance from the end of the block. Measure and remember that distance (distance *a* on *Figure 2*). Without moving the square, measure the distance from the bottom of the bowl to the square (distance *b*). Subtract distance *b* from *a* and you now know how far the bottom of the bowl is from the jaws.

For example, if the square is 5" from the end of the block (distance *a*) and the distance from the square to the bottom of the bowl is 4" (distance *b*), then, subtracting *b* from *a*, the bottom of the bowl is 1" from the jaws.

If the bowl has walls 1/4" thick and you want the foot to be 1/2" thick, then you can remove another 1/4" of wood until *a* minus *b* equals 3/4".

Finish the foot

To determine the thickness of the bowl's bottom when finishing the foot, there is one other object to make. With the jumbo jaws mounted onto the lathe, insert a ½" dowel through the spindle (the spindle of my lathe is hollow, as are most). Insert the dowel so that the end is flush with the face of the jumbo jaws. On the left end, wrap blue tape around the dowel and on that tape, permanently mark the exact location of the end of the spindle.

Mount the bowl onto the jumbo jaws so that its foot can be finished. Slide the dowel through the spindle until it touches the inside bottom of the bowl. Note on the end of the dowel the location of the end of the spindle and measure the distance from this point to the mark made on the blue tape. This is the bowl's depth, distance *x* on *Figure 3*.

Slide the block *x* distance from the base of the headstock. The end of the block is now even with the bottom of the bowl. Use a spring clamp to keep this block in place.

Set the square on the lathe a convenient distance from the end of the block, measure, and remember that distance (distance *a*). Without moving the square, measure the distance from the bowl's foot to the square (distance *b*). Subtract *b* from *a* and you know the thickness of the bowl's foot.

AW 27:3, p32

For example, if the square is 3" from the end of the block (distance *a*) and the distance from the square to the bowl's foot is 2" (distance *b*), then, *a* minus *b* indicates the bowl's foot is 1" thick. If the walls on the bowl are ¼" thick, then you have ¾" thickness for making the foot.

Spend a little time getting the dowel (used with the jumbo jaws) and the blocks of wood precisely made and they can be used for years. This method is quick and simple and has never failed me. As I'm making shavings, I'm confident I know exactly how thick the bowl bottom is and how much room I have to either increase the depth of the bowl or how thick I can make the foot.

Dick Powell is the public outreach forester for Starker Forests (starkerforests.com) and works in the forests of Oregon's Coast Range. Most of the wood he turns is scrounged from scraps that are left after a timber harvest. Dick is a member of the Willamette Valley Woodturners.

Figure 1. End view End view of block, size to lathe ways.

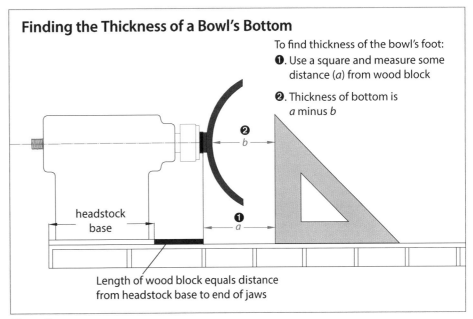

Figure 2.

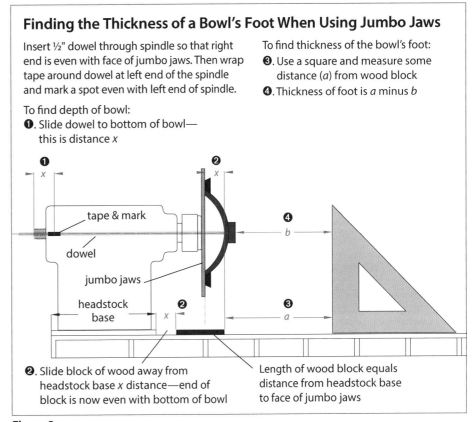

Figure 3.

Working with Burls

Mike Jackofsky

I have always been fascinated by the beauty and unique nature of burls, and turning hollow vessels seemed like a great way to take advantage of this splendid material. Over the years, most of my work has consisted of making natural-edge hollow vessels from burls.

Burl wood is generally more stable than straight-grain wood that comes from the trunk of the tree. Even so, when burls are freshly cut and still green (wet), they can be unstable, and the wood will not hold the shape after turning, as the piece dries. My solution is to let the burl dry *before* turning, at least a little bit. I store burls for six to eighteen months before I turn them. I seal the wood with greenwood sealer and keep it outdoors under a tarp to maintain a moist environment. It's important for the wood to dry slowly.

On hot, dry days, I often spray water under the tarp. A pleasant side effect is that the wood will darken and spalt, giving it more color and character. In essence, I am seasoning the wood. My objective is to dry the wood slowly enough to stabilize it, without drying it so much that it becomes difficult to work with.

I have turned many different kinds of burls over the years: buckeye, redwood, manzanita, madrone, cherry, and oak, but the wood I have used most frequently is bigleaf maple burl. I live near San Diego and bigleaf maple grows in southern Oregon. It is easily available on a consistent basis,

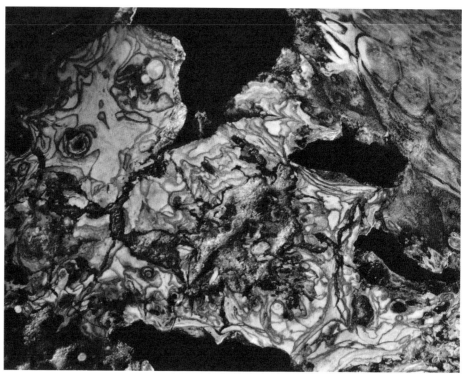

Detail of boxelder vessel with voids and bark inclusions.

and I have become familiar with its characteristics.

When maple burl has a reasonable amount of moisture in it, it will cut easily; when it becomes bone dry, the process becomes much more difficult, almost like working with a different material. I don't have a formula for my process, so I don't have a particular moisture-content percentage to offer, but my general rule is that if water is coming off the piece when it's being turned, it is too wet to hold the shape. Some turners rough-turn hollow vessels, then when the turning is dry, re-turn them to a final form. I only want to turn my hollow forms once.

Proportions

I don't adhere to any hard-and-fast rules about the proportions of the wood when I cut it up to mount onto the lathe, but I tend toward shapes that are slightly larger in diameter than in height. For example, if I cut a piece that is about 12" (30 cm) in diameter, I would want about 9" to 12" (22 cm to 30 cm) for the height.

When I teach, I like to have the students start off with a square/cube of wood—this starting point allows for a lot of flexibility as a shape is created. If you preshape the block with a saw into something that is close to what you want to make, you have already made decisions that

AW 27.2, p38

will greatly affect the final piece. I prefer to start with a cube and do my shaping on the lathe. This allows me to respond to what my bowl gouges uncover. And, by leaving more wood at the bottom of the block during the shaping process, I am able to tilt the wood at the tailstock end to manipulate the burl to the orientation I want, to take advantage of unique features in the wood.

I generally buy burls that are large, often up to 2,500 lb (1,135 kg) when green. When I cut them up with my chainsaw, I try to get them into cubes, with the center of each cube flat or slightly indented. This is where the natural-edge opening will end up. These large burls are often very irregular. The challenge is to achieve a balance between the ideal piece I want to start out with, yet avoid too much waste. In a perfect world, I would start out with a square block that has good possibilities for a beautiful natural edge in the center.

Box elder natural-edge vessel, 2010, 8" × 9" (20 cm × 23 cm)

Buckeye burl natural-edge hollow vessel, 2009, 9" × 13" (23 cm × 33 cm)

Madrone natural-edge open bowl, 2011, 10" × 12" (25 cm × 30 cm)

Mounting and turning between centers

To safely mount a piece of burl between centers, I have developed a technique that is a little different than what other turners use. I use a 1" (25 mm) two-prong spur drive to turn big pieces. I select where the opening will be, and drill a 1"-diameter hole, past the bark, and about 1/4" (6 mm) into the solid wood. This hole will solidly seat the spur drive into the wood and, in my experience, makes the process much safer. I can then take aggressive cuts, and as long as I keep checking to be sure that the live center on the tailstock end is tight, I know that the

chunk of wood is not likely to come off the lathe.

This drilled hole will become the opening of the hollow vessel; selecting its location is the first significant decision I make. I often choose a location that is not in the center of the cube—perhaps a natural edge will line up better otherwise. Deciding where to locate the opening of the hollow vessel becomes easier with years of trial-and-error experience. Sometimes, I sacrifice part of the burl and end up with a smaller vessel, but this allows more control over the shape and look of the vessel. The outcome is not simply an accident—it is my choice of how to best orient a particular piece of burl.

I turn the wood between centers until I get close to the final shape, and then I make a tenon and mount the wood into a chuck. I will then make my final decisions regarding shape.

Cutting burl with gouges

With burl, there are no uphill or downhill rules of cutting the wood to get a clean cut. The grain swirls around in unpredictable directions, which is how the burl was formed in the first place. You might end up cutting into endgrain-type material anywhere on the piece, and you will find that some parts might be cutting cleanly, while other portions are showing torn grain on the same cut. My way to deal with this is to make fine, careful cuts when I

Whole maple burl, approximately 500 lb.

Maple burl cut into a cube.

Two-prong spur drive seated into a cube of maple burl (for turning between centers).

Mike hollows a maple burl vessel.

am close to the final shape, with a freshly sharpened bowl gouge. I use push cuts with a small gouge and pull, shear cuts with a large gouge to make refinements.

While I am making my roughing cuts between centers, I try to determine in which direction the wood will cut the cleanest, so when I get to those final cuts, I have an idea of what will work best on that particular piece of burl.

Bark inclusions and voids

Burls are a bit mysterious and surprising. I find all sorts of surprises as I cut into them. Some burls, like buckeye, are root burls, and I can expect to encounter sand, pebbles, and even rocks that the burl grew around as it was forming.

I often see burl for sale with the bark removed, but I prefer to start with the bark still attached. Sometimes I use some of the bark as part of the wall of the vessel, and that can be challenging, as the bark is a completely different material from the solid wood. In that case, I often use thin CA glue, early in the process, to give more structural strength to the vessel. I also use some glue to keep pieces of the bark intact, if I think they will contribute something positive to the final piece. I rarely use CA glue to repair a piece of bark that flies off during the hollowing process, because that glue joint will most likely be too obvious. I don't want the glue to become a feature of the vessel.

I use glue almost like a piece of tape, to hold the bark in places where I want to try and keep it. But, if it is obvious that the bark is not going to cooperate and become a part of the final piece, I don't force the issue by using a lot of glue that will show up in the finished vessel.

Creating a pleasing form

One of the most challenging aspects of working with a burl is finding a balance between taking advantage of the unique features of the material and letting it totally dictate what you make. Using wood that is special to you (expensive, rare, unique) can be a trap where you value the wood to an extent that you are afraid to turn much of it away. You can be so aware of its cost or uniqueness that you believe you have to make the biggest object you can. When I have been in that frame of mind, I usually find the end result to be less than pleasing.

I don't have many rules in making my work, but I try always to "sacrifice size for form." I am much better off making a smaller piece that I find pleasing, than a slightly larger one that I think is just okay. I understand this is easy to say, because the temptation is always there to try and hang on to as much of that expensive burl as you can. Resist that urge.

Hollowing burl

Hollowing burl is not that much different than working with straight-grained woods, as long as the wood still has some moisture in it. If, however, the material is dry or if it has sand or rocks inside, that is a very different situation. I used HSS cutters for many years, and dry, hard wood with embedded sand can take a long time to hollow because a lot of time is devoted to sharpening the cutter tips. Just as with a chainsaw, as soon as the cutter touches sand or rock, it becomes dull.

I now use hollowing tools that I designed and they have carbide cutters and swivel tips. The carbide enables me to complete projects that would have been next to impossible with HSS. There are a number of hollowing tools available that use carbide cutters, and your choice of hollowing tools really comes

down to which ones you are most comfortable with. I use only hand-held hollowing tools—that enables me to experience the feel of working with the wood and the sense of freedom that allows.

When you find tools that you especially like, those are the tools you should use. If you plan on hollowing tough, hard material, though, you might want to consider using carbide cutters. They can be much more efficient than HSS for cutting burls.

I want to end up with a smooth surface anywhere a vessel can be felt. When I know that I am getting close to a final wall thickness, I slow down the cutting process to achieve a smooth, final surface. I then extend that good-quality surface into the vessel, at least where I can reach my fingers. The rest of the inside will hold up to inspection with a light, but I don't worry about the feel of the surface in a place that nobody will ever touch.

Sanding and surface quality

After I make final clean cuts with a sharp gouge (to minimize sanding) I do as much sanding as

Mesquite natural-edge hollow vessel, 2010, 9" × 8" (23 cm × 20 cm)

I have to, until I am satisfied with the surface quality.

I power sand a little bit before I hollow a vessel, but I don't try to obtain a final surface quality while the vessel is on the lathe. I initially sand with 120- and/or 180-grit discs, doing a thorough job. I also sand in reverse, especially when there are a lot of bark inclusions. When bark inclusions are present, if you sand only in one direction, the disc will hit the inclusion the same way each time and the abrasive can dig into the same place. By also sanding in reverse, the bark inclusions are hit by the sanding discs from a different direction, which helps achieve a consistent wall thickness.

As you get better and more experienced with gouges, your vessels will begin to require less sanding. Until that happens, especially with burls, sand as much as you have to. A good-quality surface finish on your vessels shows how much you care about and have pride in your work. If you are willing to spend the time and effort, even as you are learning, you can achieve professional results.

Drying and finishing

After I turn a piece, I dry it slowly in a paper or plastic bag. If I use a plastic

bag, I will check it every few days and air it out to make sure that no mold is growing. I then do all my final sanding off the lathe, after the wood is fully dry. This might sound crazy—it is not the most efficient method time-wise, but it works for me. I use a 1/4-sheet palm sander with 220- and 320-grit paper to do final sanding. Sanding this way enables me to work around the bark inclusions and get the best surface finish I can possibly achieve. Sometimes I also slightly buff the wood, but that depends on what looks best with each hollow vessel.

On most burls, I build up coats of a tung-oil finish. In working with burls that have surface imperfections like bark inclusions, I never let the oil stay on the surface as long as the directions say. To avoid shiny spots in recessed areas, I wipe the oil off fairly quickly. I then immediately use a compressed-air gun to blow the oil out of recessed places. Then I wipe the surface again. The number of coats I will build up depends on the look I want. Applying multiple coats of tung oil will give a more glossy appearance. Decide what works best for you.

Working with burls to make hollow vessels with natural edges can be very rewarding. It can also be frustrating, especially if you expect to achieve perfection the first time. Repetition and experience will get you where you want to go. I have made thousands of hollow vessels and I have yet to make a perfect one; and I know I never will. Each piece teaches me something and that makes me want to improve the next one. I recommend that you keep making pieces and critiquing the results as you progress. There is no

Buckeye burl vessel, 2010, 6" × 6" (15 cm × 15 cm). This vessel was in AAW's Roots exhibit.

Maple burl natural-edge vessel, 2008, 13" × 15" (33 cm × 38 cm). This vessel was in AAW's Maple Medley exhibit.

substitute for experience with this type of project.

One of the best "tools" to take advantage of when creating hollow vessels from burls is a sense of humor. Of course, I am always aware of safety factors, but I try not to take myself too seriously, so I remind my students that, "this isn't brain surgery." Sometimes, defects in the wood are out of your control; you might as well accept and work with them.

One of my survival techniques is not to get too attached to the piece I am working on until it is off the lathe. As far as I am concerned,

it doesn't exist until it survives the whole turning process and I am holding the finished vessel in my hands. Until then, it is just raw material and I don't hesitate to make that "one last cut" to try to get a more pleasing shape or maintain the consistency of the wall thickness.

The feeling of holding a finished piece in my hands at the end of the day, knowing that I created it from a block of wood, is for me the most enjoyable part of woodturning.

Stay safe, keep increasing your experience level, and have fun!

Mike holds a maple burl hollow vessel.

Mike Jackofsky is a full-time professional woodturner from California and a member of the San Diego Woodturners. Mike teaches and demonstrates and he designed the Hollow-Pro tools he uses in his work. To find out more about Mike, his work, and his new DVD, Woodturning with Mike Jackofsky: Making a Hollow Vessel, visit mikejackofsky.com.

Remounting Dry Bowl Blanks

David Lancaster

The most efficient way to produce bowls is to turn them green with a relatively thick wall, dry them, and re-mount and re-turn them to final wall thickness. This process allows the green wood to dry without cracking, though it does warp. The problem, then, is in remounting the warped bowl blank so that re-turning can proceed as efficiently as green turning.

Before addressing this problem, let's consider the first question of efficient green turning. The green blank can be mounted in one of several ways: between centers, with a screw center, or with a faceplate, the last being the method I use. Whichever method, we are faced with the decision: do we turn the bowl with the mounting on the bottom or the top of the bowl?

If we mount on the bottom of the bowl, in order to cut with the grain (from small diameter to large in faceplate work), we will have to turn from the left to the right. Because of the proximity of the headstock, we can't rub the bevel cutting this way—the headstock interferes with the tool handle. Instead we have to make a pulling cut, without the bevel rubbing, which is a very difficult cut to make while keeping total control. To maintain maximum control and remove a large amount of material fast and efficiently, you must rub the bevel. That's why most people, including myself, turn the bowl with its top facing the headstock. In this way you are able to turn from small to large diameters with speed and efficiency and with the bevel rubbing. You are also applying all of the pressure toward the large headstock bearings, which are designed to

Make drum chucks in a variety of sizes, top. Use them to mount dried bowl blanks, above, with the rim toward the headstock for efficient, bevel-rubbing cuts, free of headstock interference.

withstand this load, rather than the lighter tailstock bearings.

After you remove the waste from the inside of the bowl and it has been dried either by air or in a kiln, you are now ready to re-mount the bowl to finish-turn.

Now what do we do? Most common is to screw a faceplate to the base or to hold it with a chuck. If we do this, we are faced with the same problem: working in the wrong direction. To get the most efficient cuts, we must mount the bowl with its rim towards the headstock. But this dried bowl blank is warped and twisted considerably out of shape. So how do we hold it?

What I do is make a drum chuck. A drum chuck is just a cylinder of wood attached to a faceplate. It can be

as simple as a solid block or a roughed-out bowl blank or a segmented drum mounted to a faceplate. When you have completed this much of the chuck, mount the faceplate on the lathe and turn the cylinder smooth. Round off the open end to eliminate any sharp corners.

Now I apply a piece of 1/8-inch closed-cell neoprene rubber with 3M spray adhesive to the rounded end. You can make these chucks in various sizes to fit different bowls. I have them in four sizes: 3 x 3-1/2-inch dia., 3 x 5-inch dia., 4 x 7-inch dia., and one 4 x 10-inch dia. for large bowls and platters. (By the way, these chucks are also my vacuum chucks).

Now that you have made your chuck, mount your bowl to it. The chuck should fit inside the bowl somewhere between halfway down the bowl and the bottom. Absent vacuum pressure, bring the live tail-stock center into the center of the base, apply pressure with the hand-wheel, and lock the barrel.

Now you can finish-turn the outside of your bowl the easy way. You will be able to turn from the base to the rim with controlled bevel-rubbing cuts, employing continuous flowing motions without interference from the headstock.

I use an Irish grind on a 3/8-inch gouge. The first cut trues the bottom and creates a spigot to grasp with a scroll chuck when the bowl is reversed for the inside. To complete the outside, continue working from the base to the rim.

Give this approach a try. It sure has made a difference for me.

David Lancaster is a production bowl turner in Weeks Mills, ME.

AW 11:2, p18

Turn a Burl Bowl

David Lancaster, Ken Keogh

Photo: David Higgins

"David Lancaster turns a thousand bowls a year and sells them all." —from *American Woodturner* (December 1995). In the years since that statement appeared on these pages, David still turns a thousand bowls a year—sometimes up to 1,200—but now there is a significant difference in his work.

The secret to the beauty of David's burl bowls is the exquisitely fine finishing cuts that he makes both outside and inside the bowl. Tear-out is non-existent; a light burnish is often present. And when you reach the point at which you turn a thousand bowls a year—and sell them all—you will make these kinds of cuts, too.

Today, David uses less brute strength and less willful force. Smaller gouges with shorter handles have replaced heavy, long-handled gouges. Consistently well-made bowls have yielded to more refined forms made with gentler cuts. Sharp details and a mature elegance have evolved over the years.

Read on to learn how you can turn a 16"-diameter bowl using David's techniques.

AW 20:2, p46

Tools

For this project, you'll need:

- 1/2" and 3/8" Irish-grind bowl gouges
- 1/2" x 1/8" diamond-shaped shear scraper
- 1/2" shallow-flute spindle gouge ground on a bias
- 4" face plate
- four-jaw chuck
- vacuum chuck
- 10" drum chuck
- bowl-coring system

For his bowls, David likes the leverage and mobility in tight areas that curved tool rests and short-handle Hosaluk-style gouges give him.

Prepare the blank

First, select a burl

For this project, David chose from three or four burls. The most promising of these was an 18" rock maple burl with little distortion from bark inclusions and manageable spalting.

Since David's bowls usually are functional, they can't have bark inclusions that destroy their integrity as vessels. And they must be burled deeply enough to prevent an interior that is mostly tree trunk.

Mark the shape

Scribe an 18"-diameter circle to define the outside diameter of the bowl.

Rough cuts

Carefully chainsaw the circumference into a reasonably balanced bowl blank.

David uses a 16" electric chainsaw for this step, which avoids having fumes from gas-powered saws inside his shop.

Next, attach a 4" face plate to the face of the burl using an impact driver and four #10 ×1-1/4" McFeely square drive screws. Since this burl is valuable, he uses the small face plate to maximize the area where he will core two additional bowls.

Rough-turn the outside

Rough-turn the outside with a 1/2" Irish-grind gouge. The curved tool rest shown in *Figure 1* enables him to be close to the workpiece and eliminates the need for the leverage that long tool handles provide.

Establish the rough shape by creating "steps" made with bevel-rubbing plunge cuts with the flute orientation at about 10 o'clock.

The tailstock is in place throughout the outside turning process, thus the small face plate acts as a strong spur drive.

As the roughing process proceeds, a bark inclusion becomes evident as shown in *Figure 2*.

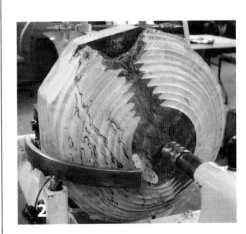

A careful assessment reveals that moving the face plate 1/2" away from the bark inclusion will allow David to remove it with little effect on the final diameter, *Figure 3*.

As the piece turns, the high side hammers on the gouge.

David recommends holding the gouge parallel to the floor, thus transferring the hammer force straight into the tool rest (*Figure 4*).

Working around the bark inclusion altered the centerpoint of the bowl's base. Be sure to re-mark the tailstock center on the face of the burl before beginning the coring process.

To refine the shape, David uses a variety of pulling and pushing cuts, but always with the bevel rubbing. David follows this straightforward design plan:

- Establish the rim.
- When satisfied with the rim, establish the foot.
- When satisfied with the foot, connect the foot and the rim with a full, smooth, harmonious curve.

Shape the rim

To create a rounded rim, cut away the material underneath the rim. This is a nice nuance that frames the beads you will turn between the rim and the body of the bowl. Refine the rim and the beads with a small diamond-shaped shear scraper. In skilled hands, this tool will roll a bead faster than you can say Richard Raffan. These beads provide an elegant detail on a large bowl (*Figure 5*).

Next, sand the beads and rim. David uses 3M Radial Bristle Discs in grits from 120 to 240. Sanding with these discs requires reversing the lathe direction to capitalize on the curve engineered into the discs (*Figure 6*).

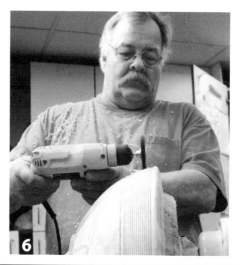

Core the bowl

The foot has been established in the form of a 4" tenon made to enable you to transfer the bowl to a four-jaw chuck. This eliminates using a faceplate and the accompanying danger of screw holes popping through the bottom or into the foot.

Before you begin coring, be prepared to lubricate the burl with water. This will simplify the coring process—especially with a dry, wild grain burl. The watering process does not require anything more sophisticated than a water bottle to squirt water into the coring cut. This lubricates and cools the burl while washing the chips out of the cut (*Figures 7, 8*).

After coring the blank, remount the bowl onto a 10" drum chuck using vacuum power. If you shifted the bowl to remove a bark inclusion (as David did in *Figure 3*), remember to align the bowl on the drum chuck with the new tailstock mark.

Now, cut away the tenon and make the final cuts to create the foot of the bowl (*Figure 9*).

Drill for depth

After finishing the foot and before turning the inside of the bowl, take the cored blank to your drill press, which is set to drill to the depth that allows you to maintain an appropriate wall thickness at the bottom of the bowl—in this case 3/8". This hole does not need to be perfectly centered—it's simply a depth stop (*Figure 10*).

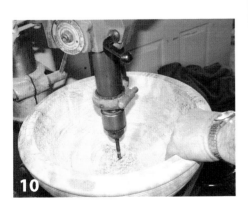

Turn the inside

Turning the inside requires a 10" drum chuck and a vacuum system. With partial vacuum pressure to support the bowl, align the blank with a dead-blow mallet. Check the distance between the rim and the tool rest while rotating the workpiece by hand (*Figure 11*).

Turn the inside of the bowl with a 3/8" Irish-grind gouge and a curved tool rest. Make your final cuts with a 1/2" shallow-flute spindle gouge, ground on a bias. David recommends gentle cuts, gentle curves, and cutting with the grain from the outside to the center.

Remove stock to the depth of the hole drilled in the blank (*Figure 12*).

Sand and finish

Sand the outside of the bowl with a 3/4" soft foam backing pad chucked in a pneumatic random orbit sander. David begins with 3M 220-grit purple paper and progresses to 320 grit. Then he switches to 3M Microfinishing Film for the final sanding.

The inside of the bowl requires a different technique to eliminate the tiny ripples that almost always appear. With the bowl held static on the lathe, use a 5" disc mounted on a 3/4" soft pad and chucked in an electric drill. If necessary, use 120-grit and 240-grit purple paper. Repeat final sanding with Microfinishing Film.

Apply a food-grade finish. David applies tung oil to all his bowls.

After completing the 16" bowl, he turned 13"- and 10"-diameter bowls from the cored pieces. The set of three had exceptional grain throughout—perhaps the best he's ever seen turned from maple burl.

David Lancaster (heirloombowls.com) of Weeks Mills, Maine, was a featured demonstrator at the 2005 AAW symposium in Overland Park. Fellow Maine woodturner Ken Keoughan (kkeoughan@yahoo.com) is a frequent contributor to American Woodturner.

Green Wood Not So Free

Clarissa Spawn

I've turned green wood exclusively for the past five years. My bowls typically range from 15"–30" (40cm–75cm) in diameter and their design often depends on the warping that occurs in the drying process. Turning large bowls from green wood and letting them warp requires substantial chunks of freshly cut wood. Size, design, and sustainability are three good reasons to turn green wood. Cost isn't one of them.

The wood used to turn *Bowl with Wire* originated from a tree in my neighbors' yard. While my husband and I were attending a Christmas party at their home, Tom commented that he was going to have a large maple removed in order to build an addition to their home. Lacking in wood, but abundant in holiday spirits, I made my usual offer,

"If you bring me your fallen tree, I will make you a bowl in return. If I have to come get it, I'll let you buy a bowl for half price." I have since then revised my offer. Harvesting wood from my neighbors' tree ended up being an expensive proposition.

Eighteen months later, Tom called my woodlot manager (a/k/a my husband Alex) to let him know the tree was down and the trunk was lying in the yard. All the branches had been removed and hauled away. Since this was a treasured tree, Tom planned to make his wife Jane a table out of the lumber milled from the trunk. He wanted to know if we would we like the stump. "Well, no," my woodlot manager replied, "but let me know if you change your mind about the log."

At this point, I was flush with wood and did not want maple,

which rots quickly once felled. But we knew we would be hearing from Tom in the near future because he had failed to consider two important points: who would mill his lumber and how he would transport it.

Lumber mills do not want yard trees because they tend to be full of foreign material, usually metallic in nature. Past finds include a turnbuckle, nails, buckshot, and a metal sign. Although sawyers with portable sawmills will often tackle yard trees, with an agreement that the log owner replace any damaged blades, there are currently no portable sawmills operating in our area. And if one were to be found, the log would have to be cut in half lengthwise to fit on a portable mill. In either case, additional large equipment would be required to load and/or transport the log.

Bowl with Wire, 2008, Maple, 5½" × 21" (140mm × 53cm)

AW 24:4, p30

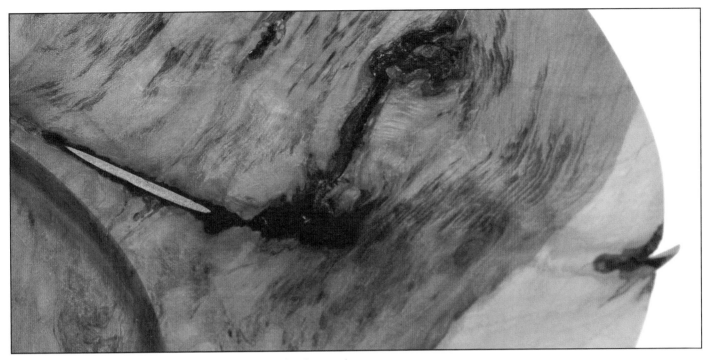

A close-up view of the 10½"-long (27cm) wire embedded in the wood.

Sure enough, we did hear back from Tom. In his view, he had something of value lying in his yard. In our view, he had a problem. Besides removing the log, he had the additional burden of having promised his wife a keepsake. So, Alex agreed to help him cut up the log. I decided to stand by my offer of a half-price bowl.

Early on a Saturday morning, we showed up at Tom and Jane's house with the thousands of dollars of equipment required to render large felled trees: a Stihl chainsaw with a 36" (90cm) bar, safety gear, cant hook and spud bar, chains and come-along, and our pickup truck. Thirty hours of labor later (five people for six hours), we had two, too-large chunks of wood in the truck and Tom and Jane had a pile of firewood in their yard.

There are costs and hazards associated with making offers to friends such as the one I made: Tom and Jane did not want to spend over $100 for a bowl, the wood contained wire, and Alex later developed poison ivy. Other options for collecting green wood (from tree service companies and burn lots) come with their own set of problems. It is important to recognize that there are costs involved with harvesting "free" wood. Weigh those costs carefully against your need and desire for the particular wood being salvaged. And, as in any business deal, be careful about entering into agreements with friends. Sometimes purchasing a log for cash can be a whole lot cheaper.

Clarissa Spawn lives and works in the bluegrass region of Kentucky. She has participated in invitational exhibits at the Kentucky Museum of Art and Craft in Louisville and the gallery at the Kentucky Artisan Center in Berea. Initially self-taught and assisted by woodturning friends, she furthered her skills through courses at Arrowmont.

Rimmed Bowls

Joshua Friend

Incorporating a rim of contrasting wood adds flair to turned bowls. I've always loved the dramatic effect of using contrasting woods together, and a bowl is a great application for achieving that look. Adding a rim is relatively simple—if you can turn a bowl, you can turn a rimmed bowl. The main challenge is to create a glue joint that will last. Here's how.

Wood selection

For dramatic effect, I like to use wood species that highly contrast with each other, such as black walnut and maple. I've also had good results combining butternut with walnut, cherry with walnut, and even cherry with pine (though nowadays I prefer hardwoods). Experiment with the woods you like to turn to see which combinations are appealing.

Equally as important as the wood species is the glue joint where the rim meets the bowl. To achieve an imperceptible-to-the-touch seam, you must use wood that is sufficiently dry. If you cut the bowl from green wood (an unseasoned log), the wood must be allowed to dry so that its shrinkage and warping can occur prior to joining with another piece of wood. This kind of wood movement—the reshaping of a rough-turned bowl that occurs during drying—would ruin any glue joint, even if you've prepared the two surfaces to mate perfectly. The other kind of wood movement—seasonal expansion and contraction that comes with changes in humidity—will not damage a well-fitted joint if the grain is oriented properly. I do not use a moisture meter to gauge a bowl's readiness, but rather notice and feel when the wood has stopped shrinking and losing water.

As with the wood for the bowl, the rim material can also be wood that you have rough turned and dried. Store-bought, kiln-dried dimensional lumber is also fine to use as either bowl or rim material, but let it sit in your shop for a few weeks before using it; even kiln-dried wood needs to acclimate to your workshop humidity and may warp and move in the process.

Glue joint basics

A woodworker once told me that "glue is your very good friend," and this is true, but keep in mind neither extra glue nor extra clamping pressure takes the place of a perfectly fitted joint. When thinking about the bowl-to-rim glue joint, the principles of joining boards edge-to-edge apply. The main difference for bowls is that the bowl-to-rim joint is a lamination (one surface on top of the other), but that distinction makes no difference, as long as you orient the grain of both parts parallel with each other.

Think of a solid-wood bowl as a board with a different shape: Instead of being flat, it has curved sides. You can still identify the direction of the grain in a bowl, just as you can in a flat board. So, before gluing the rim material to the bowl, identify the endgrain of the bowl by finding where the growth rings go around concentrically. Match the bowl's grain direction with that of the rim material (*Figure 1*). When the grain runs in the same direction, both pieces of wood expand and contract similarly. A perpendicular grain orientation would fight against the natural expansion and contraction that occurs in wood and the glue joint would eventually fail.

AW 27:2, p34

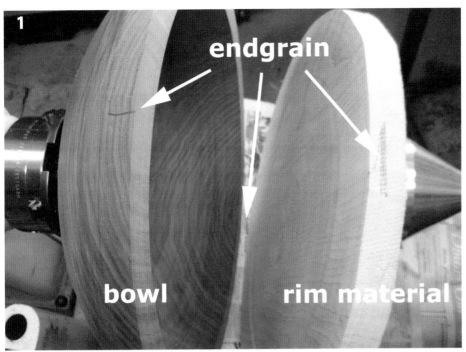

endgrain

bowl

rim material

Orient two mating surfaces so that the grain runs in the same direction.

Measure, mark, and then cut the rim material to approximate diameter. Mount the rim material onto the lathe.

I use Tightbond type II or III wood glue for water resistance and superior wood bonding. With these glues, it is not advisable to rough up the two surfaces for better adhesion (that's a myth). Also, it is sufficient to apply glue to only one of the two surfaces (not both), as long as you spread the glue thoroughly on the surface so there are no dry spots. Finally, it is not necessary to use any kind of spline or fancy glue edges such as rabbets. Well-mated, dead-flat surfaces will produce a tight, lasting joint.

Prepare the rim material

I like to use a single dry board for the rim material. Depending on the diameter of your bowl, however, it may be necessary to glue boards edge-to-edge to make a rim piece large enough. (If that's the case, you could make the joining look more intentional by inserting a detail in the glue joints.) Place the bowl onto the rim board upside down and mark the circumference of the bowl onto the rim board. Then cut out that shape, being careful to cut about ½" (13 mm) outside of your line. This extra material would be cut off later at the lathe (*Figures 2, 3*).

Mount the rim material onto the lathe to cut a flat gluing surface. For smaller-diameter pieces, it is sufficient to use a screw chuck for mounting, but larger diameters require a faceplate for better support at the outer edges where the cutting will occur. Without proper support, your cutting force can cause deflection of the wood, which will make it more difficult to create a flat surface. You do not need the entire span of the board to be flat—only the outer edges where the bowl's rim will make contact. So, identify the area you need to make flat (allowing a little extra that can be trimmed off later) and slightly undercut the center portion of the board. This will allow you to use a straightedge to get a reading of the flatness of the outer edges.

To fine-tune the surface, I like to either shear scrape with a bowl gouge turned on its side and/or use a heavy, straight scraper. Another option is to use sandpaper wrapped around a flat block (*Figures 4, 5, 6*).

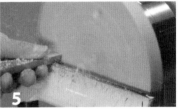

Prepare the gluing surface of the rim material with whatever method works best for you.

Use a straightedge across the entire diameter to test for flatness, not only at the rim area, but also across the entire board. It may be helpful to shine a light from under the straightedge to highlight any gaps.

8 Mount the rough-turned bowl onto the lathe. A jam chuck along with the tailstock for support works well. Turn the tenon and outer walls back into round.

9 Remount the bowl into the 4-jaw chuck and turn the rim dead flat in preparation for gluing on the rim material.

10

11 Minor adjustments to the bowl's rim and to the rim material can be made by hand sanding against a surface you know is flat.

When testing for flatness, it is not enough to test only one section of the rim material at a time; you may find that area to be flat, but it also must be flat in relation to the opposing rim across the board's diameter. Therefore, hold the straightedge across the whole piece and seek flatness at both ends. Continue to take small amounts and turn off the lathe to test the rim board until you have achieved flatness in the area that is to be joined to the bowl (*Figure 7*).

Prepare the bowl

If you are using a bowl that you have rough turned and dried from green wood (as opposed to store-bought, kiln-dried wood), first mount it onto the lathe for truing the outside. This step is necessary because the bowl may still have a wax emulsion sealer on it, and the bowl and tenon will have moved out of round during the drying process. To mount a dried, rough-turned bowl, I use a jam chuck with the tailstock brought up for support (*Figure 8*). The interior of the bowl is placed over a scrap block that has been mounted and turned to an appropriate size and shape of the bowl, but generally a bit smaller than the diameter of the bowl. If your bowl is small enough, sometimes the chuck itself can be used inside the bowl instead of a scrap block.

Use sufficient pressure from the tailstock to trap the bowl securely against the jam chuck. With the bowl in this orientation, true the tenon and the outside of the bowl.

Remove the bowl and remount it by grabbing the trued tenon in a 4-jaw chuck so that the rim and inside of the bowl can be cut. For now, only cut the inside enough to remove the wax sealer and bring the bowl into round. Leave the walls thick enough to final-turn later,

after the contrasting rim has been glued on.

If you are using dimensional lumber for the bowl material, the outside truing process is probably not necessary. Simply mount your bowl into the chuck so the rim can be prepared. The object is to cut the rim so that it is dead flat across the entire bowl. As with the rim material, test for absolute flatness with a straightedge held across the diameter of the bowl. Fine-tune the

12

13

14

15

Various clamping methods can be used.

rim surface until you have achieved flatness (*Figures 9, 10*).

Dry-fit the bowl and rim material by holding them together with the grain running in the same direction (parallel). If adjustments need to be made, now is the time, either on the lathe again or, if your bowl is small enough, by sanding the piece using a full sheet of 80-grit paper against a dead flat surface (*Figure 11*). When you are satisfied with the dry fit, it's time for glue-up.

Clamping methods

It's been said that the lathe is a very expensive clamp, and indeed it is a great tool for clamping the rim to the bowl. Other clamping methods include applying weight with a heavy object such as a sandbag, clamping across boards, using deep-throated clamps, or using a drillpress by raising the table height to press the pieces together (*Figures 12, 13, 14, 15*). I've had success with all of these methods. Remember, though, that you don't need excessive clamping pressure if you have created a well-fitted joint—just enough to get a little glue squeeze-out all the way around the bowl.

Finish-turn the bowl

After the glue has cured (at least 24 hours in most cases), you can begin finish-turning your rimmed bowl. Start by mounting the bowl by its tenon into a 4-jaw chuck. Turn away the center portion of the rim material. I do this with a parting tool, cutting straight in so that the remaining waste disk can be used as rim material for another, smaller bowl (*Figure 16*). Slow down the lathe's speed as you near the end of this cut so the disk does not fly off when you cut through. In fact, I like to turn the lathe off and pull the disk off by hand (*Figure 17*).

Finish-turn and sand the bowl as you normally would (*Figures 18, 19, 20*). Apply the finish of your choice and enjoy your new creation.

Joshua Friend, a woodturner and writer, is a member of the Nutmeg Woodturners League, an AAW chapter that meets in Brookfield, CT. See jfriendwoodworks. com for examples of his work and contact information.

A parting tool is perfect for removing the center part of the rim material, which can be used on another, smaller bowl.

Finish-turn your bowl.

Platter with Burned Rim

Nick Cook

My fascination with fire started in 1993 at the AAW symposium in Purchase, New York. I watched Australian Vic Wood burn the rim of a platter, and I was immediately hooked.

At first, I thought it would be a great way to avoid having to sand. Boy, was I wrong. You really need to carefully sand the surface before you start the burn. Otherwise, it will end up looking like you didn't spend enough time sanding the platter.

Since watching Vic, I have turned and burned literally hundreds of plates and platters. I have used ash, cherry, maple, myrtle, and oak. All hardwoods work well but my favorite is ash. The grain and figure of ash works superbly with the burning process, and it is usually available in larger widths and more affordable prices for platter work.

I think you will like the effects of the black burned rim against the creamy natural color of the interior of the piece. I also like the contrast between the undulations of the rim and the smooth surface of the interior.

Tools and turning stock

I primarily turn this project with a 3/8" deep-fluted bowl gouge with a side grind and a 3/8" bedan tool.

You'll need a screw chuck and a 4-jaw chuck. I prefer the Jerry Glaser screw chucks because the threads are cut deeper and are considerably sharper than any other I have used. For this size platter, I like the security that a 1/2" chuck provides better than a 1/4".

I always start with kiln-dried lumber. Green wood and even air-dried blocks are less stable. They are more likely to check and crack and will certainly distort more than dry wood. Thicker stock is also better; the heat will radically distort thin material.

For this article, select 8/4 ash, 12" wide. With a compass, lay out the 12"-diameter circle. Then cut a round disc on the bandsaw. Determine which side will be the face or top of the finished piece and drill a 3/8" hole in the center for a screw chuck.

Turn the outside

First, attach the blank to the screw chuck and make sure the face of the chuck fits snugly against the blank. If not, the blank will not run true. Mount the screw chuck onto your lathe.

AW 20:2, p50

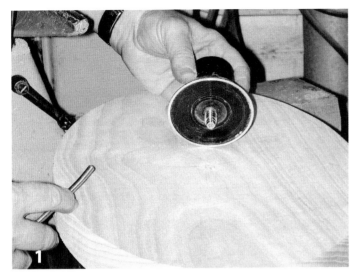

After cutting the round blank, mount a 1/2" screw chuck in the center. Check that the chuck fits snugly against the blank.

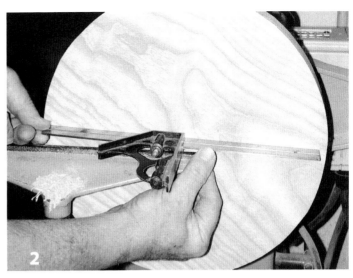

After turning the surface flat with a 3/8" deep-fluted bowl gouge, check for flatness with a 12" combination square.

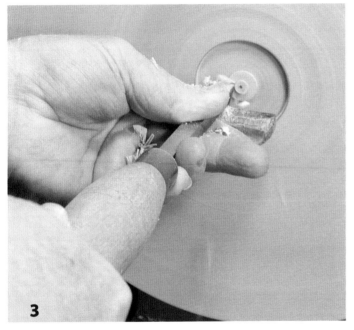

With a 3/8" bedan tool, cut the scroll-chuck recess. Many turners believe a slightly convex bottom has strong eye appeal.

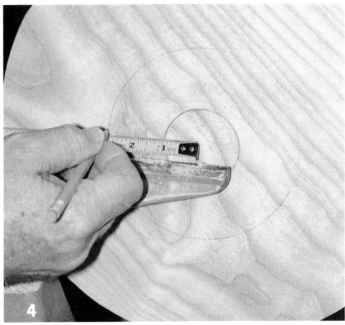

To mark off the foot of the plate, scribe a 5-1/2"- to 6"-diameter circle. The foot should be about one half the platter diameter.

Next, position the tool rest at 90 degrees to the axis of the lathe, just below the center and about 1/4" from the face of the blank. Rotate the piece by hand to ensure clearance. Start the lathe at 750 to 1000 rpm for roughing the blank with a 3/8" deep-fluted bowl gouge.

Hold the bowl gouge tool handle down with the flute almost upright and place the bevel parallel to the surface you plan to leave. Start your first cut at the rim and finish at the center of the blank. One to three very light cuts should flatten the surface and produce a flat starting point. This cut is especially important if you're turning rough-sawn material.

Once the surface is flat, locate and mark the center. I use a vernier scale or compass to scribe a 2"-diameter circle for the recess to accommodate my scroll chuck. Then cut the recess with a 3/8" bedan tool. Rather than making the recess flat, I usually make the bottom slightly convex, leaving it just a little higher in the center than the perimeter. In my eyes, this looks better than a flat surface.

After cutting the recess, scribe a 5-1/2"- to 6"-diameter circle for the foot of the 12" piece. On a plate or platter, I try to make the foot approximately one half the overall diameter of the piece. (Less than half will make the finished piece a little top heavy and less stable.)

Shape the bottom

It is important at this point to create a curve from the beginning. If you start making straight cuts, you will leave little room to form a continuous curve from the foot to the rim. I use the same 3/8" bowl gouge to shape the bottom.

Set the tool rest at 45 degrees and at the edge of the work piece. Hold the handle downward, with the flute at about 45 degrees and start the cut about 1/2" in from the edge of the platter.

Each cut is made with your body—not with your hands. I keep the handle perpendicular to the surface being cut and against my body. Start each cut a little closer to the foot and make each cut toward the rim. Continue making successive cuts until you have one curve from the foot to within 1/8" of the rim. Use the tip of the tool to define the foot.

For variety, try straight, chamfered, and curved feet. I lean toward the chamfered foot for most of my platters.

After shaping the bottom of the piece, make finishing cuts to get rid of tear-out, ridges, and uneven surfaces. I use the longest part of the bevel on the same 3/8" bowl gouge to make this type of finishing cut. Here's how.

Hold the tool in an almost vertical position with the handle against your thigh for support. Then lay the heel of the bevel against the wood. With absolutely no pressure at all, pull the tool from the foot to the rim. This cut will produce what I refer to as angel-hair shavings that will flow down the flute of the tool. This shearing action will leave about as fine a surface as you can produce with a tool. It also reduces the amount of sanding required. To make ridges more visible, place a light directly over the blank.

With a 3/8" bowl gouge, keep the handle perpendicular to the surface. The tool rest is positioned at 45 degrees.

Use the tip of your bowl gouge to define the perimeter of the platter's foot. This photo shows detailing a chamfered foot.

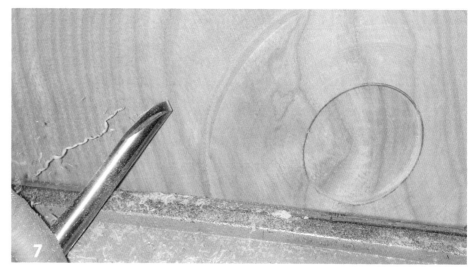

With your thigh as support, hold the bowl gouge nearly vertical to make finishing cuts. When you rest the heel of the bevel against the wood, you should see fine angel-hair shavings peeling off the platter.

Sand the bottom

Once you're satisfied with the surface, start sanding. I prefer a power-sanding technique with a fairly stiff pad. (I have learned that using softer pads on ash and other open-grain woods produces an undulated surface.) I turn the lathe speed down to about 500 rpm for sanding.

If you executed a good finishing cut, you should be able to start with 150-grit sandpaper; coarser grits will cause deep sanding marks that are hard to remove. Work your way through 180 grit and finish up with 220 grit on the power sanding.

I also sand the surface by hand with the grain, without the lathe running to get rid of any cross-grain sanding marks. Remove the blank from the screw chuck.

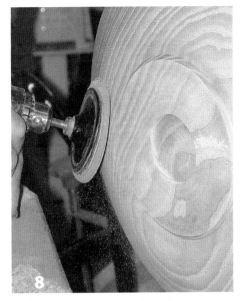

With the lathe running at about 500 rpm, begin power-sanding the platter bottom with a stiff 3"-diameter pad.

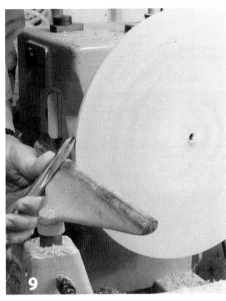

To produce a clean rim, hold the bowl gouge nearly vertical. The gouge flute should face right.

Lightly tighten the scroll-chuck jaws in the recess. To check for proper seating, rotate the chuck before fully tightening.

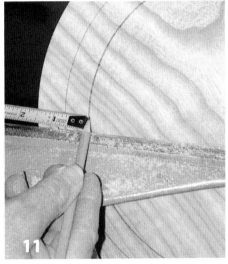

On the lathe, lay out a 1-1/2"-wide rim. This platter will have a crown centered about 3/4" from the platter's edge.

Turn the rim

Place the blank facedown on the bed of your lathe. Fully close the jaws of the chuck and insert it into the recess. Lightly tighten the chuck, then rotate it within the recess to make sure it is properly seated. Once seated, fully tighten the chuck. Screw the chuck onto your lathe.

Place the tool rest parallel to the axis of the lathe, just below center and 1/4" from the edge of the blank. Rotate the blank by hand to ensure clearance. Make several light cuts from the back to the face of the piece with the bowl gouge handle almost vertical and the flute facing to the right. This should produce a clean surface.

Avoid lifting the handle, as it can catch the end grain and cause the edge to split off. Always cut from left to right to avoid tear-out on the underside of the piece, which you've already finish-sanded. Also avoid checking the piece with your finger when the lathe is running—you're liable to get cut. Stop the machine and inspect the surface visually. Make sure you remove all saw marks.

Rotate the tool rest across the face of the piece, just below center and 1/4" from the surface. Make the same cut from rim to center that you used for the platter bottom. Several light cuts should flatten the surface.

Now, determine the width and shape of your rim. On this 12" piece, a 1-1/2"-wide rim looks nice. My favorite shape is a slight crown. To plan this, measure in 1-1/2" from the edge, then make a pencil line and another just 3/4" from the edge, which will be the crown of the rim.

Creating the crown is just like rolling a bead. You can do this with any one of several tools. I continue turning with the same 3/8" bowl gouge.

Roll your gouge to the right from the centerline and then roll the tool to the left from the centerline—just remember to leave the centerline. Place the bevel against the surface at the centerline and gently lift the handle. Roll the tool first to the right and then to the left. Use extreme care to avoid making the edge of the rim too thin. If it starts getting thin, flatten it again.

Here is where your technique will vary from turning a traditional platter. Rather than going ahead and opening the interior of the piece, continue to work with the rim. Power-sand the crowned rim with 150-, 180-, and finally 220-grit sandpaper. Then hand sand the surface with the grain to eliminate cross-sanding marks.

Burn the rim

With that done, you must thoroughly clear all the shavings and dust from the lathe and blow the dust from the blank.

I use a propane torch for my burning. I've tried Mapp gas but found it burns too hot for this detailing work.

You'll also need a container of clean water and a medium-grit 3M Scotchbrite pad. To keep water off your lathe, cover the ways with plastic bags. Be sure to have a fire extinguisher close at hand.

Do not attempt to burn the piece with the lathe running! Ignite the torch and start by lightly waving the flame over the surface. Always direct the flame toward the perimeter of the piece to avoid having it burn the outer surface of the rim.

The first thing you will see is the summer growth or softer grain turning dark. This is a nice effect if you can do it evenly. The surface will start to look similar to zebra wood. I prefer to continue to burn the surface deeper.

As the surface gets hotter and darkens, it may catch fire. Do not panic! Grab the Scotchbrite pad, dip it in the water, and wet the surface. This will extinguish the flame. The more you burn, the more you will learn how close to the surface and how long to leave the flame in one spot.

Use the handwheel to rotate the piece as you continue to burn. Once you have uniformly blackened the rim, cut back the surface with the Scotchbrite pad. This will abrade into the softer grain and leave the harder areas standing higher.

I repeat the process until the surface pleases my eyes. The final rim should appear to have uniform undulations over the surface. At this point, you may wish to make V cuts through the burned rim to reveal the wood's original, unburned color.

Turn the interior

Position the tool rest across the face of the piece, just below the center and about 1/4" from the face. From here on, the technique is just like it is for any other plate or platter.

Place the tip of your bowl gouge on the surface just to the left of the center hole. The flute should be facing in, with the handle level and at approximately 45 degrees across the face of the piece. As you break through the surface with the tool tip, roll the flute upright and pull the handle around toward you in an arch while maintaining its level position. This will keep the bevel supporting the cut as you make one continuous curve through the platter interior.

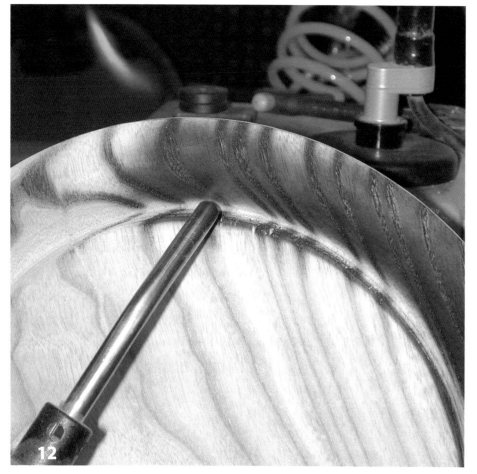

With a propane torch, begin scorching the platter rim. The tip of the flame gently kisses the freshly turned rim.

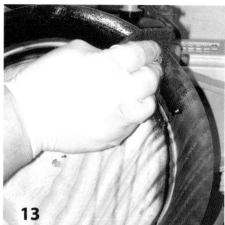

After burning the entire rim, cut back the scorched ash with a medium-grit 3M Scotchbrite pad dipped in water. Soft grain will abrade first.

14

As you approach the rim, take lighter cuts with the bowl gouge. This will ensure a crisp line at the rim.

15

Power-sand the interior with a 3"- diameter pad. It's a good idea to sand domestic hardwoods to 220 grit.

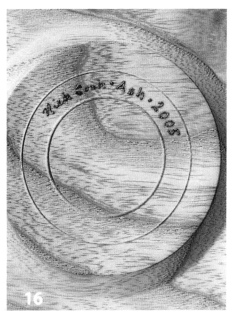

16

Two lines about 1/4" apart in the recess will provide you with an excellent place to sign your platter.

Continue with consecutive light cuts as you work out toward the rim. Avoid taking heavy cuts that may cause tear-out in the end-grain areas. As you near the rim, take lighter cuts to ensure a clean line between the rim and the interior. You can also under-cut the rim slightly to give the appearance of more depth.

Power-sand to 220 grit. I've found that sanding beyond 220 grit on most domestic woods is usually a waste of time prior to the application of the first coat of finish or sealer. (You may continue through 400 grit or even higher after the wood is sealed.)

Remove the chuck marks

After thoroughly sanding the piece, remove it from the chuck. You can use a variety of methods to remove all indications of the expanding chuck on the bottom.

One of the easiest techniques is to use the oversize or jumbo jaws that are available for most scroll chucks. You can also use a jam chuck or a vacuum chuck.

There are also several details that will enhance the bottom of the

piece. I like to keep it simple and just remove the straight recess by chamfering it slightly inward toward the center.

Scribe two lines within the recess about 1/4" apart. This gives you a place to sign and date your work. I prefer a signature tip on a burning tool to sign my pieces.

Apply finish

My favorite finish on burned pieces is a clear flat or matte lacquer. This will intensify the depth of the charred wood by eliminating any sheen.

Your most important task is to get rid of all the sanding dust. Thoroughly blow out any dust on or in the surface of the rim; a small speck of dust on the burned rim will show up like a sore thumb.

Nick Cook is a professional woodturner living in Marietta, Georgia. Find out more at nickcookwoodturner.com. He demonstrated this project at the AAW 2005 symposium in Overland Park, KS.

Two-Piece Hollow Vessel

Brian McEvoy

When turning one-piece hollow forms, woodturners rely on many methods, tools, and jigs. Success is a challenge—even for experienced woodturners.

But switch to my two-part turning approach, and your chances for success will improve dramatically:

• **No additional tools required.** Just sharpen the tools you currently use to turn a platter or a bowl—this project requires no special hollowing tools.

• **Thin is in.** Wall thickness is not an issue. You can easily turn a piece to 1/8" thickness or less.

• **Smooth inside.** With this approach, you can completely finish the inside. And when your friends or customers poke their fingers inside the opening (you know they will), they will not get a sliver.

• **Safe makes sense.** One-piece hollowing requires risky techniques. Hanging a gouge or scraper a long way over a tool rest is a precarious technique. My two-part approach improves safety.

To succeed, I recommend you have the skill to turn two similar shallow bowls.

I have completed hollow forms over 20" in diameter and only 4" deep. Because I pierce much of my work, I turn most of these forms to less than 1/8" thick. I am not sure this would be possible with any other method. Because of the simplicity, I can comfortably turn three or four 10"- to 12"-diameter forms in a day. And they are good sellers for me. Give it a try. The results can be stunning.

Get started

For turning tools, you will need 1/4" and 5/8" bowl gouges and a 1" skew. For your lathe, you'll need a 4" faceplate, a four-jaw chuck, and

"Peace Offering." Box elder; 3×12". Grouse feather design with braided deer hide and antique trading beads.

Photos: Linda Finstad and Cheryl Lowry

AW 21:3, p30

Turn the outside top

1 At your bandsaw, cut the blank in two. If you are unable to cut a slab this size at your bandsaw, use two pieces from the same board of even-grained stock. I have good results with a 1" skip-tooth blade (3 tpi).

2 Cut the pieces round and attach 4" faceplates to what will become the inside of the saucer. (You can complete this with one faceplate.)

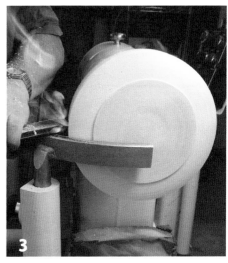

3 Select the best or most interesting grain for the top. Turn this section first.

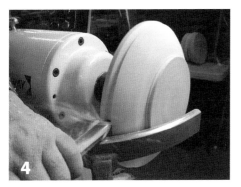

4 Use care not to reduce the diameter of either the top or the bottom pieces. Remember that they must match perfectly.

5 Finish turning the outside profile of the top section. Turn a 3/4"- to 1"-deep recess for what will become the top opening. Be mindful of the position of the screws holding the faceplate.

6 Using the technique you prefer for completing a bowl, turn a dovetail inside the top opening. You'll use this to mount the four-jaw chuck jaws during reverse turning. The top outside is complete for now. It is not necessary to sand at this point.

a cone center. If you don't have access to a cone center, turn a similar profile for a live center. (You'll find cone centers that can provide a guide for turning the shape in most turning catalogs.)

Choose well-seasoned lumber for this project—your stock must be dry to about 6 percent. If you have a moisture meter, it would be wise to take a reading after bandsawing the stock in Step 1.

For this project, I selected a piece of 3 × 12 × 12" box elder.

When you complete turning and embellishing the surface, apply a finish of your choice. In my shop, I spray on four or five coats of lacquer finish.

Brian McEvoy (onegoodturn.ca) is a studio turner who lives in Edmonton, Alberta.

Turn the bottom

To turn the outside of the bottom section of the saucer, repeat the profiling steps.

Turn a foot with a 1/4" recess for rechucking in a later step. The depth of the recess is the primary difference between the bottom and the top pieces.

Sand the foot inside and outside to finished standards (500 grit in my shop). Next, remove the faceplates from both halves.

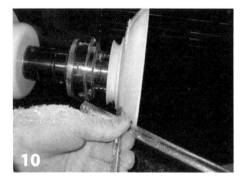

Mount the top section into a four-jaw chuck. I prefer extended-jaw models, which provide extra room for my tools.

If your piece is the slightest bit out of round, gently re-turn and true up the surface. Remove as little material from the outside edge as possible.

Square the inside edge of the top. Remove only the stock necessary to square the face—you do not want to lose too much in diameter.

With a gouge, remove enough material to get a straightedge across the full diameter without hitting high spots.

With a steel straightedge, check that the outside lip is perfectly flat. Remember that this will be your glue joint.

For final turning, use a 1" skew turned on its side.

Once you are sure the edge is perfectly flat (a 1/4"-wide glue joint is fine), begin hollowing the inside.

Alaskan yellow cedar; 5 × 21 × 1/16".

This is one of Brian's largest hollow forms. It features pyrography and pierced feathers.

Turn the inside top

17

Now, turn the top to 1/8" thickness. Remove the stock in 1" stages, starting from the outside edge. Achieve the proper thickness in each 1" segment before moving to the center.

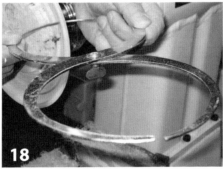

18

Use a caliper to accurately measure the thickness throughout the top.

19

Continue removing material in 1" steps. A sharp tool and a firm yet relaxed grip will prevent chatter.

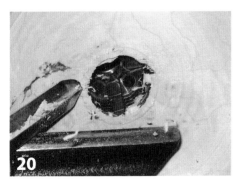

20

Eventually you will break through the deep recess in the top piece. This becomes the inside of the top opening.

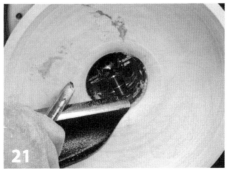

21

Thoroughly clean up the top opening, being careful not to hit the chuck jaws—leave 1/16" to 1/8" of wood surrounding the jaws. You will later sand away this stock.

22

Sand the inside to 320-grit smoothness. Curious handlers can't resist feeling the inside, so do a thorough job.

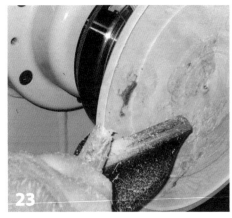

After removing the top half from the chuck, mount the bottom half and repeat the steps completed for the top portion. Remember to true the 1/4" lip perfectly; this becomes a glue joint.

You're now ready for a dry test. Gently tweak the joint if necessary. A slight variance (1/16" or less) in the diameter of the two sections is acceptable—your final sanding and finishing will take care of discrepancies.

Finish turning the inside of the bottom section until the thickness matches that of the top. Sand to your finishing standards.

While it's still mounted on the lathe, apply a clear finish (I prefer clear lacquer) to the inside bottom section. Be careful not to get any finish on the 1/4"-wide glue joint.

Keep the bottom half mounted on the lathe. Test the fit again by finding the best bookmatch position. To make assembly easier, use a pencil to mark the match on both pieces.

Apply yellow woodworker's glue to the 1/4"-wide rim on both pieces. Remove excess glue.

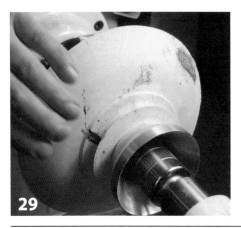

Using a cone center, line up the pencil marks and clamp the two pieces, using the tailstock to apply pressure. If a cone center is not in your arsenal, turn one to fit your live center and size it to match the opening on the top section.

30

During clamping, the cone will center the top half to match the bottom. Exert enough pressure to squeeze out the glue. Then clean up the excess and clamp for 15 to 20 minutes or as recommended on the glue bottle.

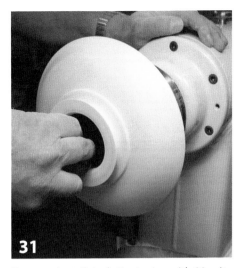

31

Remove the tailstock. Beginning with 80-grit sandpaper, finish up the opening. (I have good results with a Swiss-made foam-backed sandpaper.)

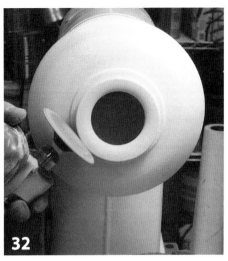

32

Finish-sand the top and bottom with handheld or power techniques that you favor. I sand my pieces to 500-grit smoothness.

"Acoma Seed Jar." Alaskan yellow cedar and acrylic paint; 4 × 7". The Mimbres, an ancient American Southwest tribe, provided the inspiration for the design of this two-piece hollow form.

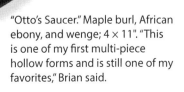

"Otto's Saucer." Maple burl, African ebony, and wenge; 4 × 11". "This is one of my first multi-piece hollow forms and is still one of my favorites," Brian said.

Bowl Bottoms

Thomas Trager

When the bottom of a vessel, bowl, or box contributes to the presentation of the piece, the result can be spectacular. But do we spend as much time designing the bottoms of our turned objects as we do the rest of the piece? Bases support our work and offer an opportunity for a pleasant surprise.

Design

Form and function are primary to design. Two other considerations play a role, especially when designing bottoms: interest or surprise and space for a signature. If all of these elements are carefully thought out in the design stage, the bottom will naturally complement the vessel, function is ensured, interest or surprise exists, and space is available for a signature.

Lift is an aspect to think about when designing the bottom of a bowl or vessel. Lift gives a sense of lightness to a vessel as it sits on a table or display stand. Lift can be subtle or overt. In the vessel by Bert Marsh, the foot is distinctively tall, which adds lightness and delicacy. Bert Marsh tells us, "My vases and bowls are organic in concept and the foot plays an important part in the overall appearance. The foot lifts them up from the substrate as if they had burst through and blossomed."

Lift can be implied subtly by simply rounding over the side of the bowl where it meets the bottom or by incorporating a tiny foot hidden underneath the bottom, slightly elevating the object *(Figure 1)*.

Perhaps the look you want to achieve is one of being grounded. In that case, a flat, wide bottom is called for, maybe just slightly rounding the edge of a box, as the side flows into the bottom.

Bottoms are not just about lift—they serve a function by supporting the object. If the intent is for the object to remain stable, design

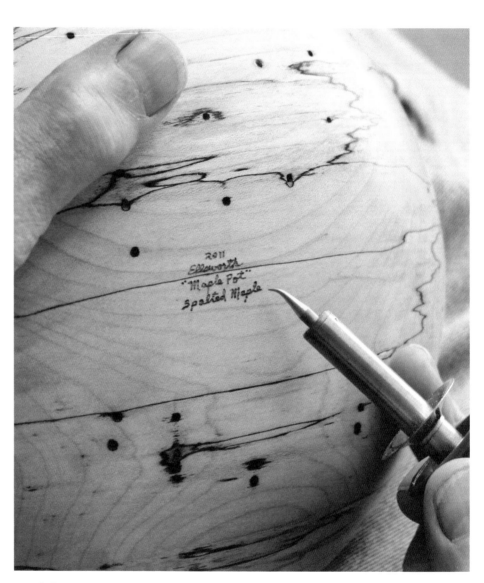

David Ellsworth signs his turnings on the bottom, using a wood burner. He bends the tip slightly to make it easier to use.

AW 26:5, p31

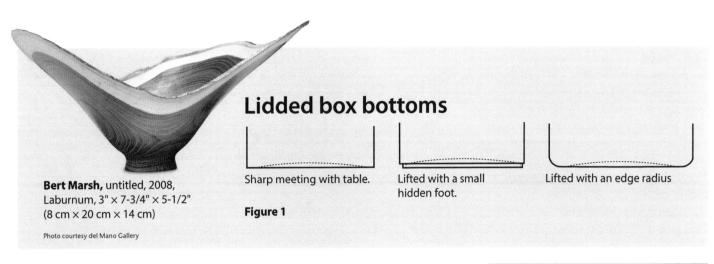

Lidded box bottoms

Sharp meeting with table.

Lifted with a small hidden foot.

Lifted with an edge radius

Figure 1

Bert Marsh, untitled, 2008, Laburnum, 3" × 7-3/4" × 5-1/2" (8 cm × 20 cm × 14 cm)

Photo courtesy del Mano Gallery

accordingly. A stable, wide base is appropriate for a salad bowl. Goblets should not be tippy. On the other hand, a popcorn or ice cream bowl might feel just right if the bottom is rounded for cradling in someone's hand or lap.

Although function might seem to strictly dictate the form of a vessel's bottom, serving a function does not necessarily inhibit creativity. For instance, a large bottom on a functional vessel offers ample space for detailing. Instability can intentionally be incorporated into function. Who says a candy or nut bowl has to have a flat bottom? A rounded bowl, heavily weighted in its bottom, will tip and wobble as people reach for goodies, then wobble upright again.

The makers

Most of Binh Pho's vessels have a graceful sweep upward from their bases. There is a sense of lightness as the pieces seemingly float. Binh also solidly grounds some of his

work, such as *Three Goats in the Fairy Tale* where the vessel was inverted, the opening becoming the base. Binh states, "My pieces often do not have a foot. I carefully tuck in the bottom, following the curve of the vessel. The diameter of the bottom depends on the curve of the vessel. In general, the bottom is quite small, from half an inch to two inches. My belief is that a vessel or bowl does not need a foot, unless the foot means something to the piece. For sculptural pieces, sometimes a large, flat bottom is required—the foot now becomes part of the design. Signature space is not important; I can find a spot somewhere on the piece to sign. An artist's true signature is the appearance of the piece."

Molly Winton's vessels also illustrate attention to the flow of the body upward from the base. They are finished cleanly with a bit of transition detailing added. Molly says of her approach, "When I decide on the size of a bottom,

Binh Pho, *Three Goats in the Fairy Tale*, 2007, Boxelder, acrylic paint, gold leaf, 13" × 6-1/2" × 8" (13 cm × 17 cm × 20 cm)

Eugene Schlaak, untitled, 2011, Cherry, 7-1/2" × 18" (19 cm × 47 cm)

I created the design on the rim and bottom with a Sorby texturing tool. It only takes seconds. I used a wire brush to remove the fuzz, followed by slight sanding. The engraving of my name and type of wood was done with a high-speed rotary tool with a fine carbide burr.

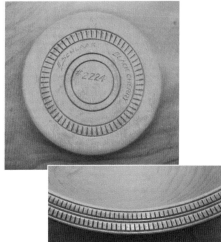

it's based on its ratio to the entire piece. I don't have a specific formula, but as I trim the base, the most critical component is to ensure that the curve follows through to the very bottom, without changing or altering the primary curve (see *Figure 2*). I want the base to appear to tuck under, which visually provides lift. I want to avoid the appearance of the piece melting into the table, or sprouting from it. I prefer a concave area for the base. Because my bases are usually fairly small, I don't do anything except outline them with a groove and add my signature and possibly the wood species."

Simplicity, grace, and purity of form are important to David Ellsworth. David says, "I design the base of my forms with the same feeling of simplicity as the forms themselves. In particular, I don't want the base to interrupt or alter the volume of the line of the base."

Interest or surprise

Ron Fleming's work superbly illustrates the thoughtfulness that can be given to the bottom of a vessel or platter. His designs flow from underneath, curling upward and outward, the bottom integral to the whole. Ron says this concept came to him quite simply, "I had a collector ask me what the bottom of one of my pieces looked like. After thinking about his question, I now start the design from the center of the bottom and evolve outward and upward."

Ingenious solution

Malcolm Zander creates delicate hollow vessels and thin-walled bowls that have flaring rims. Both forms balance ever so precariously on tiny bases. How do these fragile objects stay upright? Malcolm inserts a small rare-earth magnet in the bottom, concealed by a wooden plug. The vessels come complete with acrylic or other bases with a complementary

Molly Winton, *Buffalo Hunt Series*, 2009, Maple burl, 7" × 5-1/2" (18 cm × 14 cm)

Desirable

The sweep of the outer wall continues through space cleanly, never exiting through the bottom of the foot.

Figure 2

Ron Fleming, *Fern Basket*, 2007, Redwood burl, 21" × 19-1/2" (53 cm × 50 cm)

Ron Fleming,
Fern Platter, 2006,
Redwood burl, 3" × 24"
(8 cm × 61 cm)

Sharon Doughtie, *Nurture*, 2009,
Norfolk Island pine, 2-1/4" × 6-3/4"
(6 cm × 17 cm)

Malcolm Zander, *Leaves in a Golden Wind*, 2008, Black walnut, 23k gold leaf, 9-1/2" × 15-1/2" × 11-1/2" (24 cm × 39 cm × 29 cm)

Malcolm Zander, *Laceruffle 2*,
2008, Spalted beech, 5" × 3"
(13 cm × 7.5 cm)

magnet. Function is cleverly satisfied; lift and elegance remain.

Carved feet

Feet offer the opportunity to suggest gesture, imply character, and add elegance. They provide elevated support for a bowl or vessel and serve to lighten the overall look. The addition of feet usually creates a break in the continuous surface from the side to the bottom of a vessel *(Figure 3)*. How well that transition takes place—the curvature of the upper surface through the plane where material is left for carving individual feet and the transition to underneath the vessel—can make or break a piece. Awkward transitions will remain awkward, no matter how much carving or texturing is applied.

Sharon Doughtie incorporates feet into many of her pieces, splendidly combining their flair and curve with the vessel's shape and surface design. Sharon tells us, "I like carved feet for natural-edged bowls. They are cohesive with the organic look and feel of wavy edges." In her work, it is clear that Sharon matches the design of the bottom to the overall intent and form on a case-by-case basis. *Tweedle Tea* offers an intentional cartoon-character impression, so she designed feet with a wide stance to support that look. In the case of *Nurture*, a small base provides lift and complements the traditional form of the bowl.

Stephen Hatcher's footed teapots and vessels entail a high degree of design and planning to obtain the graceful curvature and flow between the feet and body. Stephen tells us, "Every part of a woodturning matters and the foot presents the piece, providing lift and stability. Two of the designs I've provided are examples of fairly dramatic and prominent feet."

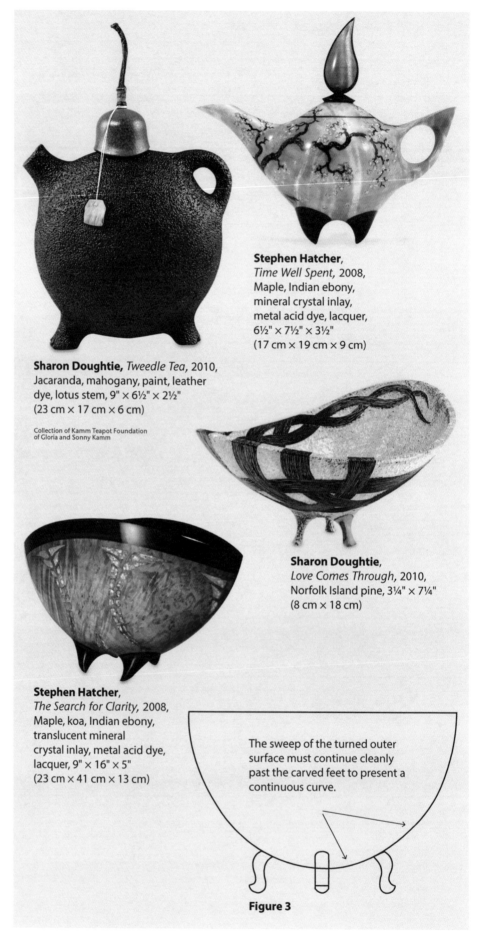

Stephen Hatcher, *Time Well Spent*, 2008, Maple, Indian ebony, mineral crystal inlay, metal acid dye, lacquer, 6½" × 7½" × 3½" (17 cm × 19 cm × 9 cm)

Sharon Doughtie, *Tweedle Tea*, 2010, Jacaranda, mahogany, paint, leather dye, lotus stem, 9" × 6½" × 2½" (23 cm × 17 cm × 6 cm)

Collection of Kamm Teapot Foundation of Gloria and Sonny Kamm

Sharon Doughtie, *Love Comes Through*, 2010, Norfolk Island pine, 3¼" × 7¼" (8 cm × 18 cm)

Stephen Hatcher, *The Search for Clarity*, 2008, Maple, koa, Indian ebony, translucent mineral crystal inlay, metal acid dye, lacquer, 9" × 16" × 5" (23 cm × 41 cm × 13 cm)

The sweep of the turned outer surface must continue cleanly past the carved feet to present a continuous curve.

Figure 3

Bill Ooms, *Sugar Bowl*, 2011, Cocobolo, African blackwood, amboyna burl, 3-1/4" × 1-3/4" dia. (8 cm × 4 cm)

"While visiting my brother Bob (also a woodturner), we enjoyed talking about the shapes of objects we saw. At breakfast, we spent a lot of time discussing the shape of a glass sugar bowl, which was the inspiration for this piece." —Bill Ooms

Signature

Your signature, refined or not, is part of your character. If you scrawl, go ahead and scrawl your name. Decide if you want to use just your initials or your complete name. While initials are easier to inscribe, they do not provide much clue to the maker. If presenting an heirloom piece to a family member, your full name might be appreciated years from now. If you sell your work, develop a signature style, and then be consistent with applying it. If there is enough space available, you might add the year the piece was made and the type of wood.

Many woodturners use an electric engraver to sign their work. Some use a wood-burning pen. Others choose a permanent marker. Each instrument has advantages and disadvantages. An electric engraver will create a signature that will be permanent, as do wood burners; however, unless you are proficient with a wood burner and also have the correct tip, a signature can easily become messy. Practice first on a piece of scrap wood from the same species as the original bowl.

Permanent markers are not always permanent. Some inks smear when finish is applied over them. On the other hand, a pen is easy to write with. Place your signature in an area that receives little wear, and even a signature with a pen will last a long time.

I love exploring what lies underneath a nicely turned bowl or vessel. Feet delight me! There is a sense of completeness when I discover a bottom that naturally contributes to the whole. Like icing on a cake, finishing a bottom is usually the last step before presenting our work for others to admire. Make your design decisions deliberate, whether simple or elaborate.

Thomas Trager discovered the joys of woodturning from a pen-turning class taught by Bill Grumbine. He is a member of the Bucks County Woodturners.

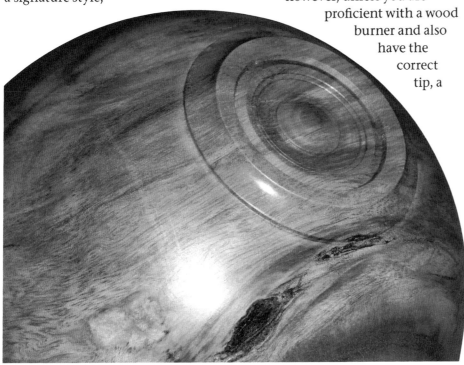

Thomas Trager, untitled, 2000, 7" × 7" (18 cm × 18 cm)

Gallery of Platters

If your vision of a platter is flat, round, and smooth, it's time to adjust your sights. These pages represent an international collection from woodturners who continue to push the rim to redefine platterwork.

Represented here are pieces from Dewey Garrett, Livermore, California; Harvey Fein, New York City; Ted Gaty, Salem, Oregon; Stephen Hatcher, Everett, Washington; Ron Layport, Pittsburgh, Pennsylvania; David Nittmann, Boulder, Colorado.

Also, Frank Penta, Chapel Hill, North Carolina; Merryll Saylan, San Rafael, California; David Schweitzer, Shelton, Washington; Al Stirt, Enosburg Falls, Vermont.

International turners represented include: Irene Grafert, Skaarup, Denmark; Robert Howard, Brisbane, Queensland, Australia; Vaughn Richmond, Warwick, Western Australia.

shapes

Platters can be square, round, free-form, or a combination of them all.

Square Ceremonial Bowl by Al Stirt, 27" x 2" x 1/2" . "The inspiration for the shape was mostly from a ceramic piece by Tony Hepburn with some of Jim Partidge's 'Blood Vessels' in mind also. The piece was turned in its square shape, from mahogany carved with rotary tools, painted with black milk paint and then sanded a bit to let some color through. The texture is a further development of some things I've been working on for many years."

Fan Tale by Vaughn Richmond, 12-3/8" x 3-1/4". "The fan is one of the most beautiful shapes in nature. This represents the Lyrebird, or leaf form of a palm tree."

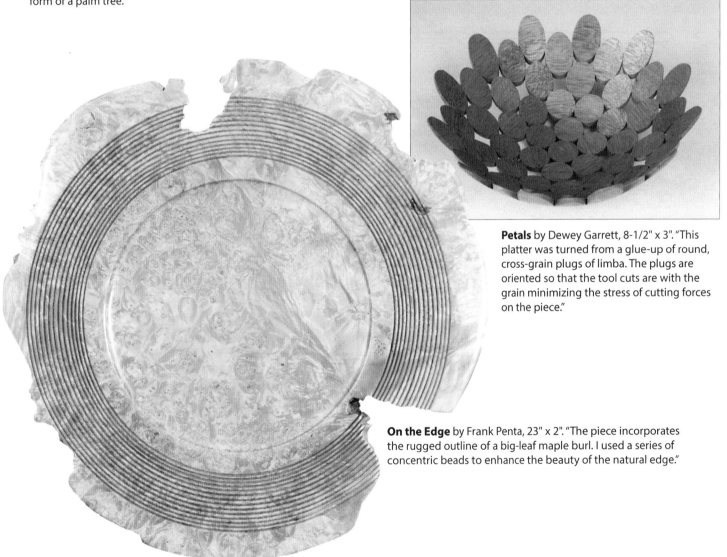

Petals by Dewey Garrett, 8-1/2" x 3". "This platter was turned from a glue-up of round, cross-grain plugs of limba. The plugs are oriented so that the tool cuts are with the grain minimizing the stress of cutting forces on the piece."

On the Edge by Frank Penta, 23" x 2". "The piece incorporates the rugged outline of a big-leaf maple burl. I used a series of concentric beads to enhance the beauty of the natural edge."

patterns

Eyes are riveted on platters with repeats.

Star Coral by Al Stirt, 17" x 2". "The pattern is a stylized version of a star coral drawn by Ernst Haeckel in the late 1800s or early 1900s. It's mahogany painted with black gesso and then carved."

Pima Flats by David Nittmann, 26" diameter. "This design is an adaptation of my 'Pima Pinwheel' piece, originally inspired by a Pima Indian's dream. It's decorated on both sides and has a custom stand that allows the piece to be displayed in either direction."

Haboki by David Nittmann, 26" diameter. "Haboki is Japanese for feather brush. This design was inspired by a family crest worn on a kimono. The single sweeping feather triggered my response. It's turned from 12/4 African mahogany."

textures

Turners expand the tactile appeal of their work.

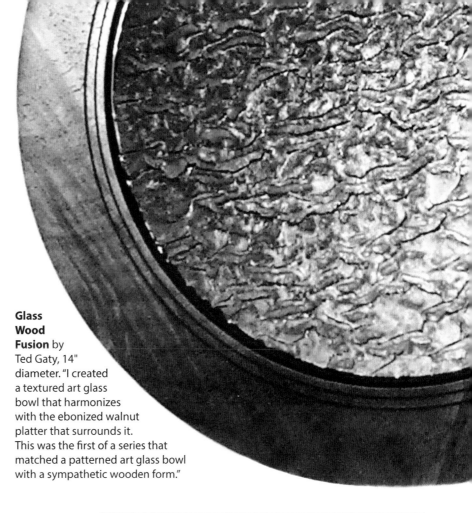

Shoreline by Merryll Saylan, 28" x 2". "Color and patterns resonate in my work from living near the shore. Color becomes more patternly—a bit uncomfortable, moving away from black."

Glass Wood Fusion by Ted Gaty, 14" diameter. "I created a textured art glass bowl that harmonizes with the ebonized walnut platter that surrounds it. This was the first of a series that matched a patterned art glass bowl with a sympathetic wooden form."

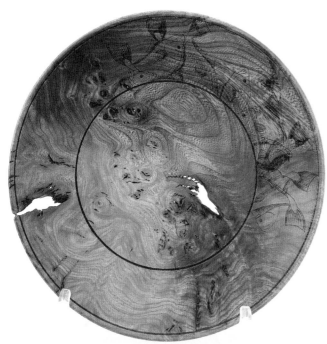

Softness by Irene Grafert, 16-1/2" x 2". "This piece had some great pattern on one side. As the other side was plain, I was inspired to add my favorite fish in a soft, discreet way."

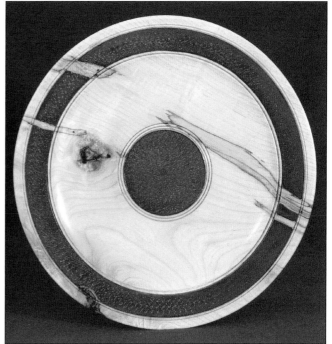

Ambrosia by Frank Penta, 15" x 2". "The textured rim and center complement the natural flow of the ambrosia pattern on this maple platter. Black gesso painted over the texturing brings out the highlights in the ambrosia."

design

Surface treatments and incorporating new materials expand the appeal of platters.

Spring Arrives by Stephen Hatcher, 18" x 3". "This curly figured maple is inlaid with crystals of green and honey calcite with accents of black mica and pink dolomite."

Moon Platter by David Schweitzer, 14" diameter. "The inspiration came while walking from my residence to my studio one evening with a sliver of the moon in the sky. I applied what I saw to the platter."

Fish, Fish, Fish.... by Irene Grafert, 161/2" x 2". "A love for bright colors, soft curves and this moving fish makes me smile and feel happy. I just had to combine all three in this platter."

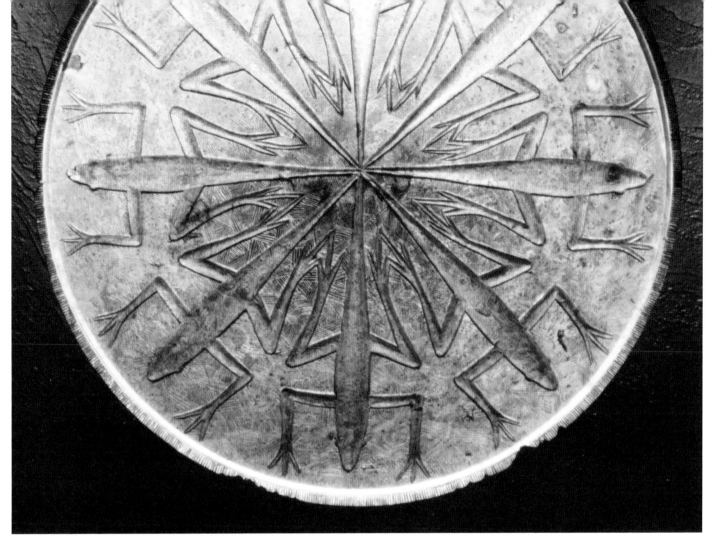

Walhalla, by Ron Layport, 16" x 3-3/4". "I drew the inspiration of this from Walhalla Plateau, a peninsula of sorts surrounded on three sides by the Grand Canyon. Here you can actually touch the morning stillness and hear the sound of the sun as it pounds out the day's heat."

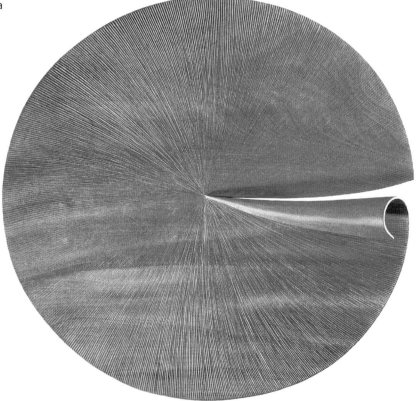

Unfurled by Robert Howard, 28" x 4". "I have had this design in my sketch book for quite a while, and it represents my love of simple, pure forms. It is a development of a previous pair of bowls that I did. The two earlier bowls differ in the treatment of the way the two curls finish in the bottom of the bowl—a small thing I guess, but important to me."

slices

Platters can feel light and airy.

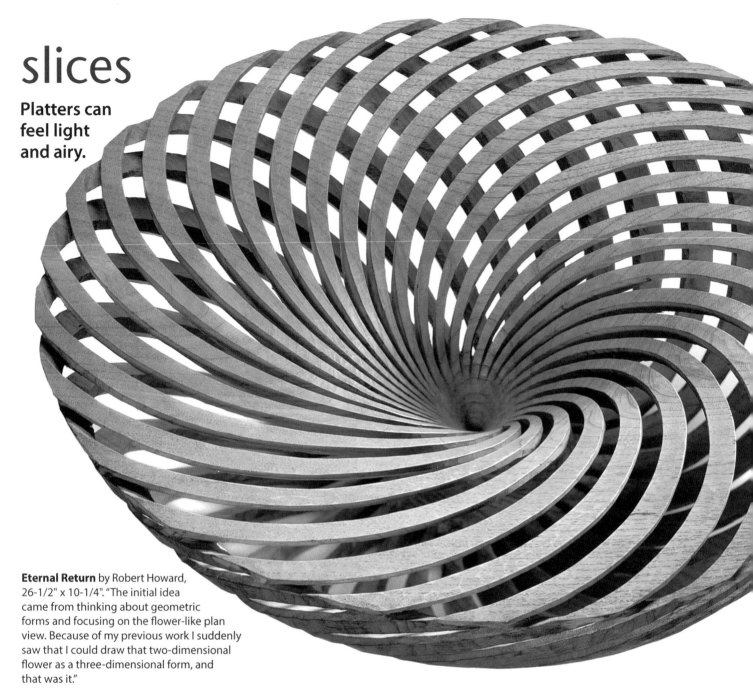

Eternal Return by Robert Howard, 26-1/2" x 10-1/4". "The initial idea came from thinking about geometric forms and focusing on the flower-like plan view. Because of my previous work I suddenly saw that I could draw that two-dimensional flower as a three-dimensional form, and that was it."

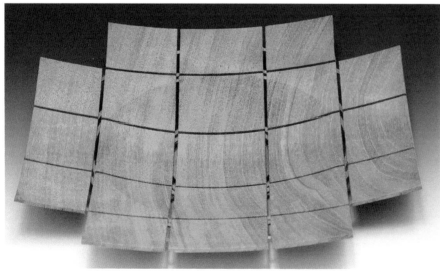

Circle in the Squares by Harvey Fein, 12-1/8" x 1-7/8". "This originally was a 10"-diameter platter called 'Four Squares.' As so often happens, in the process of reworking the design on a large scale, the idea of creating a round bowl within the platter just showed up."

Untitled Exercise in Geometry by Harvey Fein, 11-3/4" x 2".
"The title says it all—lots of sketches and no glue."

Moiré Platter by Dewey Garrett, 10-1/2" x 2". "Turned from an assembly of slats and spacers, this platter reveals the skeletal structure of a simple form. The moiré effect makes for interesting views when the observer changes position."

Platter Bases

Frank B. Penta

latters offer an excellent opportunity to express yourself creatively and to use an infinite number of designs and detailing. I have found that designing and detailing the bases on my platters is as enjoyable as executing the front of the platter.

There are two types of bases that I use frequently: a three-footed base and a multi-centered base. Here are the steps that I use to create and detail each of these base types. The three-footed base is a traditional favorite; John Uteck of the North Carolina Woodturners introduced me to multi-center bases.

Turn the platter front

With both your three-footed or multi-centered base (shown on the next page) completed and detailed, proceed to turn the front of the platter as desired. You can remount the blank on the lathe by expanding the chuck jaws into the recess in the foot of the platter.

Expanding chuck

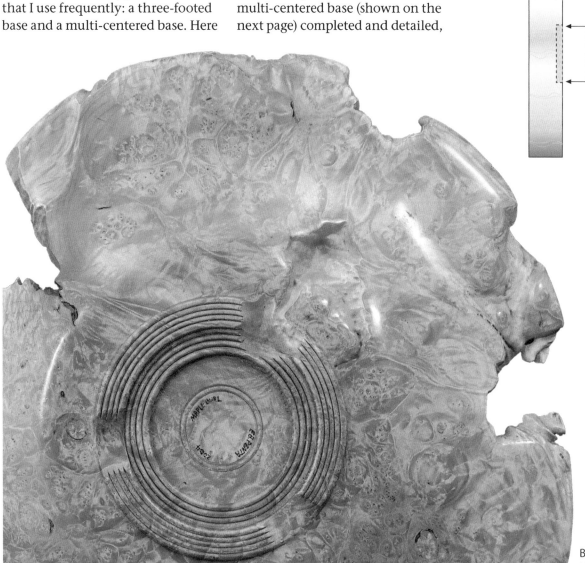

Bottom of Big Leaf Maple platter.

AW 20:1, p44

Three–footed base with detailing

Prepare the recess and foot

Once you have selected and prepared the platter blank and mounted a faceplate or screw chuck, you are ready to turn in the base. This involves preparing the recess and foot, turning the foot and base of the platter, and then detailing the base.

1. Draw 4-1/2"- and 6-1/2"-diameter circles in the center of the face of the blank, which creates a 1"-wide band.

2. Draw a 5-1/2"-diameter dotted circle in the center of the band.

3. Divide the 5-1/2"-diameter circle into thirds as shown in the drawing below.

4. Mark a line 3/4" on both sides of the three points on the band.

5. Mount the platter blank on the lathe and true it up.

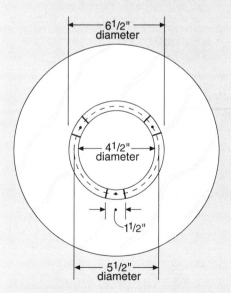

The radius of a circle is equal to about 1/6th of the circumference.

Turn the foot and base

1. Recess the 4-1/2"-diameter circle to a depth of 3/16". You will use this for expansion chucking.

2. Rough-turn the shape of the rest of the base of the platter from the 6-1/2"-diameter circle to the edge of the blank. I like to create a slight ogee near the edge of the blank.

3. Carve the three feet in the 1" band. I use a reciprocating carver and a 1" drum sander to carve the feet as shown below.

4. Refine the shape of the platter base.

5. Sand the recess foot and base of the platter to 400 grit.

6. At this point, I detail the foot, base, and recess of the platter. I use a three-point tool to turn beads and a texturing tool to texture between the beads.

7. Carefully fine-sand the completed detailing to 600 grit.

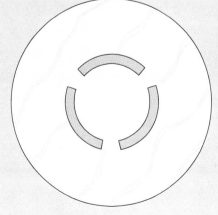

8. Remove the blank from the lathe.

9. Remove the faceplate from the blank. You are now ready to work on the front of the platter.

To shape the back of the platter, I prefer a 3/8" bowl gouge with a fingernail grind. I get less tearout when I use a pulling and slicing cut. For my finishing cuts, I use a 3/8" bowl gouge with an English grind that Allan Batty taught me.

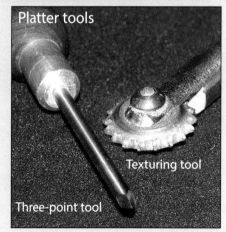

Platter tools

Texturing tool

Three-point tool

Multi-centered base with detailing

Prepare the platter front

1. Draw a 2" circle in the center of the platter front.

2. Divide the circumference into thirds.

3. Drill holes for your screw chuck in the center of the platter and at three points on the circle. Number the points 1, 2, and 3 as shown below.

4. Use a screw chuck in the center hole to mount the platter blank on the lathe and true it up.

Turn the base and bottom

1. Draw a 9" circle on the bottom of the platter.

2. Turn the shape of the rest of the bottom and sand from the 9" circle to the edge of the blank, leaving the 9" circle 1/2" higher than the rest of the base.

3. Draw 3-1/2"- and 4-1/2"-diameter circles on the base.

4. Turn a 1/4"-deep channel between the circles.

5. Sand and texture the channel.

6. Remount the platter blank in hole #1.

7. With a live center in the tailstock, mark a new center on the base.

8. Draw 5-1/2"- and 6-1/2"-diameter circles around this new center.

9. Turn a 1/4"-deep channel between these circles.

10. Sand and texture the channel. The new channel should coincide with the first channel where they overlap.

11. Repeat steps 7–10 with holes #2 and #3.

12. Remount the blank in the primary center hole and turn away the marks made with the live center on the base.

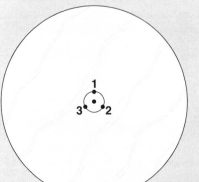

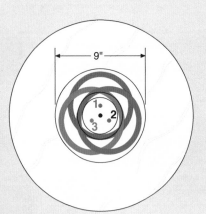

Finish the platter

No matter which of the bases you select, proper finishing will preserve and enhance both the base and the completed platter.

When adding color, I use water-based metalized dyes, inks, and transparent acrylics before the finish.

I finish my platters with an oil/varnish mix or a lacquer. I prefer oil/varnish on dark woods and lacquer on light woods. My oil/varnish mix consists of one-third pure tung oil, one-third polyurethane and one-third mineral spirits.

Frank Penta of Chapel Hill, North Carolina, is an educator and frequent turning demonstrator. His website is Woodspriteturnings.com.

Small Kiln

Bob Rosand

When I was turning a lot of pens and laminated bowls a decade ago, I built a drying chamber to alleviate problems with high moisture content. I constructed my mini-kiln from 2"-thick panels of rigid insulation and shelving material.

Inside my kiln (described in the Fall 1995 issue of *American Woodturner*), two 60-watt lightbulbs raised the temperature to 90° F while a small fan circulated the air and evenly lowered the moisture content of my turning stock. The kiln dried up my problems with cracked laminated pieces and destroyed penturning stock. It worked, but in retrospect, my homemade kiln was inefficient and certainly not a thing of beauty.

My homemade kiln didn't make the move to my new shop, primarily because I shifted to turning projects with fewer moisture-content issues. Additionally, I routinely waxed my green turned bowls and allowed them to air dry.

However, that all changed when I recently noticed a few slightly warped pieces in my shop—just enough that it was noticeable. I also had trouble with the lids fitting on some of my boxes; the wood had shrunk just enough to give an improper fit.

But it took 6" of floodwater in our basement to set a real plan in action for a new kiln. Although the floodwater wiped out my upright freezer, I had the makings of a new mini-kiln before me. And the best news: It only took me about an hour to get my freezer converted to a kiln.

My new kiln (about 2×2×4' on the interior) had shelves and was well-insulated. All I had to do was drill a dozen or so ½" vent holes in the top and sides to allow the air to circulate a bit. (Note: When drilling holes in the freezer walls, be careful to avoid drilling into cooling lines for obvious reasons.) I epoxied an inexpensive thermometer to the inside wall of my former freezer, which allows me to keep track of the temperature. I also drilled a 3/8" hole through the wall so I could put a duplex outlet inside the kiln for a light and desk-size fan.

The first thing I noticed was that a 60-watt bulb raised the temperature in the kiln to well over 100° F. I replaced that bulb with a 40-watt bulb and later a 20-watt bulb to get the temperature down to about 90° F. (I've learned that higher temperatures produce cracked turning stock.)

What I really like is that I can now dry green bowls and small and large boxes in a few days to minimize warping. Most of my pieces dry down to 6 percent in about a week. (I verify moisture content with a moisture meter.)

If you decide to build a kiln from a freezer or refrigerator, you can find discarded models at junkyards and appliance stores. The supplies and modifications described *above* will give you a small yet functional drying unit that will last for years.

Bob Rosand (rrosand.com) of Bloomsburg, Pennsylvania, is a professional turner and educator and frequent contributor to American Woodturner.

AW 22:3, p51